CHRISTINE OSTLER

DYSLEXIA

A Parents' Survival Guide

'Your words,' quoth the dragon, 'I don't understand.'
('The Dragon of Wantley' – Anon.)

AMMONITE BOOKS
GODALMING

First published 1991
2nd revised edition 1999
Reprinted 2003, 2005, 2007, 2009
© Christine Ostler 1991, 1999

Ammonite Books
58 Coopers Rise
Godalming
Surrey GU7 2NJ

ISBN 978 1 869866 13 6 (2nd edition)
ISBN 978 1 869866 06 8 (1st edition)

Printed and bound in the United Kingdom by
MPG Books Ltd, Bodmin, Cornwall.

ACKNOWLEDGEMENTS

My thanks go to Richard Dyson, who introduced me to the world of dyslexia;

to Dr Harry Chasty and Jean Walker, who trained me as a dyslexia teacher;

to Jeanette Dormer and Frances Ward for their constructive criticism;

to Sue Whitehead, for her help with the chapter on Maths.;

to Catherine Vinton, one of my pupils, for the illustrations;

to my children, Katharine and Nicholas, for their help with proof-reading, for putting up with microwaved meals, and for their helpful comments, such as, "Oh Mum! You can't write that. No-one will know what you mean!'';

to my husband, Stephen, for his encouragement and confidence that I could do it;

and especially to Jonathan, for letting me write about him so candidly.

C.A.O.

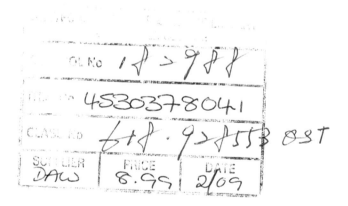

For my mother, Dorothy Winter,
with love.

CONTENTS

INTRODUCTION

FAMILY HISTORY

I am sure that Katharine, our first baby, had read all of the childcare books before she was born. I knew nothing about babies and so she was brought up 'by the book'. She co-operated beautifully, sleeping between feeds, and gurgling contentedly when awake. I would feed her whilst watching the six o'clock news; then she would be in bed by seven and we would have supper in peace and quiet. A quick feed at eleven o'clock on our way to bed and then we heard no more from her before six o'clock the next morning. Until she was about two and a half she continued having a day-time nap so that I could put my feet up with a cup of tea and a magazine.

I had trained as an infant teacher, very much into educational toys, and Katharine was supplied with a wide variety of these. She learned how to pile bricks, post shapes into holes, do jigsaws, and draw pictures; she could recite the alphabet at four years old and learned to read soon after. She loved being sung to and learned all the nursery rhymes at an early age. She could speak fluently in well-formed sentences by two and a half.

Jonathan was born when Katharine was twenty-one months old. He had most definitely not read all the baby books! He knew nothing about waiting four hours between feeds and demanded food almost non-stop (at seventeen he's not much different!). He cried all evening and we would eat supper pushing his carrycot backwards and forwards. We were told that it was three-month colic, but his sense of time was poor and it lasted until he was six months old.

He never slept past five in the morning. Eventually we solved this problem when he was quite young by teaching him to get his own breakfast. He refused to have a daytime sleep, preferring to sleep on the floor and to catnap when he felt like it. We would often find him behind the settee or under the table where he had just flopped on top of his toys and gone to sleep. He hated my singing to him and would hold his hand firmly over my mouth to stop me. He didn't say a word until he was two and a half, and that was 'Womble', his favourite television programme. The Wombles were little furry creatures who wandered over Wimbledon Common collecting rubbish. That programme has a lot to answer for, as will become clear later in this book.

He certainly wasn't going to use any of the educational toys in the way they were intended; instead, constructional games and jigsaws were often used for making pretend bonfires (it took hours to sort the jigsaws out at the end of the day). He was much happier playing with the contents of the wastepaper basket. On one occasion I remember thinking that he had turned over a new leaf. I had left him in his playpen with a selection of toys whilst I went into another room. It occurred to me that he was very quiet and I assumed, rather optimistically, that he had become absorbed playing with one of his toys. On returning to see what he was busily engaged in, I discovered that he had managed to reach through the bars of the playpen and get hold of a box of tissues; he had very carefully removed all the tissues one at a time.

On another occasion, I was in the living room feeding his younger brother and I could hear a strange 'plop, plop' sound coming from the kitchen. On investigating, I discovered that he had managed to climb onto a kitchen chair to reach the work surface, and was dropping the contents of a box of eggs one by one onto the floor. Was this the experience that got him interested in physics?

Events like this were a daily occurrence with Jonathan. At first I assumed that it was because he was a boy; I had studied sufficient child psychology to know that boys and girls developed differently and at varying speeds. It wasn't until Nicholas was born when Jonathan was nineteen months old that I realized that a difference in sex was not the complete explanation. Nicholas had obviously read the same books as Katharine and was perfectly happy to conform with daytime naps and educational toys. Jonathan was definitely different. That is not to say that he wasn't bright like his brother

14

and sister: he was very able in many ways, it was just that he did not conform to my preconceived ideas of how a young child should develop.

At five his speech was still very indistinct and only intelligible to close members of the family. After two years of nursery education and a year at infant school, he could recognise only twenty words and could count to thirteen. We couldn't understand why he was finding it so difficult to learn to read and count. When he was eight, I trained as a teacher with the Dyslexia Institute and it then became evident that he fitted the criteria for a diagnosis of dyslexia. This was confirmed by Dr Harry Chasty, the Director of the Dyslexia Institute, when Jonathan was eleven. (It also became evident that I was dyslexic as well, but that is another story!)

Having a dyslexic in the family is not easy (Katharine says having two dyslexics in the family is even worse!). A headmaster with a dyslexic son was once heard to say that "bringing up a dyslexic is an art unto itself".
There are numerous books that describe the phenomenon of dyslexia/specific learning difficulties. They examine the possible causes of dyslexia, diagnostic techniques and remediation programmes; but few books seem to tackle the problem of living with a dyslexic in the family and surviving! The purpose of this book is to fill the gap.

Many parents have asked, "What can I do at home to help?" In reply to this question I have run short 'survival' courses to share my own experiences of bringing-up a dyslexic son and to pass on strategies that I have found useful. One parent commented half-way through a course, "But this is just common sense!" and so it is. There is nothing revolutionary in what I suggest. However, the 'common-sense' approach I advocate must become a way of life and followed through over a long period. The objective is that *the dyslexic will become better organized, self-sufficient, more confident and less forgetful.* The strategies need to be developed gradually over a number of years if they are to be of any lasting value. I hope that this book might help you develop the art of bringing up your dyslexic.

CHAPTER 1

THE PROBLEM

"He's* so disorganized/untidy/forgetful."

"His shoelaces are always undone."

"What a mess his school bag is in!"

"Doesn't he know the difference between Tuesday and Thursday?"

"I only asked him to buy three items at the shop; he couldn't even remember one."

"Oh no! He hasn't lost his trainers again?"

These are the frequent cries of parents, teachers and other adults who come into daily contact with dyslexic children. Very often these problems are thought of as being quite separate from those of learning to read and spell; in fact, they are all part of being dyslexic.

WHAT IS DYSLEXIA?

There is much debate as to what dyslexia/specific learning difficulties is, or even if such a phenomenon exists, and, if it does, whether it is appropriate to give it a name. The bibliography at the end of this book gives suggested reading if you would like to explore these ideas further. I do not intend going into great detail in trying to answer these questions. However, the following definition may be helpful:

Dyslexia is (1) an organizing difficulty
(2) a memory difficulty
(3) a word-finding difficulty

Difficulties in these areas play havoc with the acquisition of literacy and numeracy skills, and are at the heart of what can make living with a dyslexic so frustrating.

What I mean by these three difficulties will become clearer as you progress through the book.

The word 'dyslexia' means 'difficulty with words'. The definition above suggests a problem that is about more than just reading and spelling and so it may not be the most suitable term to use. Many educationalists prefer the term 'specific learning difficulties': when this term is used the highly specific nature of the pupil's difficulties is identified e.g. poor short-term

---

* 'he' is used throughout for ease of reading, and because the dyslexic I know best is male.

visual or auditory memory, difficulty with blending letter-sounds into words, and so on. This can be very useful, especially when devising a remedial programme. However, for the purpose of this book I am taking a holistic ('all-round whole person') look at what the Americans would call 'the learning disabled child', and I find the term 'dyslexia' (with all its short-comings) more appropriate (it is also shorter!).

SO YOU THINK YOUR CHILD'S DYSLEXIC . . .

If your child is not progressing in reading and writing at the rate you would expect, you might wonder whether he is dyslexic. Over the last few years there has been an enormous explosion in the publicity dyslexia has received. Numerous actors, sportsmen, politicians and writers have been happy to disclose their difficulties with literacy; no self-respecting television 'soap' is without its dyslexic character. With this heightened public awareness it is to be expected that an increasing number of parents will look more closely at their child if he appears to be floundering at school.

WHAT SHOULD YOU DO?

If you are worried about your child's lack of progress it is essential that you arrange to see his teacher/s and headteacher to discuss the problems. It is possible that they will be aware of the situation and will be able to explain what they are doing, or plan to do, to remedy the learning difficulties. Depending on the size of the school and the age of the pupil, this may be achieved through the resources of the school, or the headteacher may need to bring in additional expertise from a learning support system.

The school may be able to carry out their own assessment, or it may call in a specialist teacher, or the school's psychologist.

ASSESSMENT

The assessment will probably look at what literacy skills have been mastered and will assess whether these fall within the average range, or whether the pupil is behind. His ability to solve problems, to use language and to perform non-verbally may be assessed: a discrepancy in the scores between various problem-solving activities is thought to indicate specific learning difficulties. His visual and auditory short-term memory may be measured: deficits in memory are usually associated with learning difficulties.

Ask to have the assessment results explained to you. It should then be clear whether you are worrying unnecessarily or whether there is a genuine problem. If the latter is the case, it may not be referred to as dyslexia but rather as a *specific learning difficulty*. It doesn't really matter what label is used, providing the problem is recognized and appropriate remedial plans are made.

If you are not satisfied with the assessment and wish to have a second opinion you can arrange a private assessment with an educational psychologist. A fee would be charged. It is advisable to ensure that the psychologist is recognised by the British Psychological Society, as not all psychologists are specifically trained to carry out educational assessments. A full psychological assessment should not be repeated within six months.

LIAISING WITH SCHOOL

Liaising with your dyslexic's school is a delicate operation. It is essential that you ensure that all his teachers are aware of his difficulties, whilst not giving the impression that you lack confidence in their professional integrity or competence (even if you do). Teachers are fragile creatures: I know — I am one. They can be very quick to take offence at any suggestion that their pupils could be taught in a different way or that information or advice from some other agency might be useful. This is a shame — doctors seem willing enough to seek a second opinion from a specialist if any of their patients are not responding to treatment. Ideally, teachers should be just as willing to seek advice if a pupil is not progressing appropriately. Classroom teachers do not have all the answers: they cannot be experts in every area of learning. They shouldn't expect it of themselves and parents certainly shouldn't expect it of them. However, most teachers are keen to extend their skills, so if you are a governor of your child's school, try to bring pressure to bear to ensure that in-service training in all areas of education (not just special needs) is high on the school's list of priorities.

You should not assume that information that has been recorded by your child's previous school, or that you have given to the school, about the nature of your dyslexic's learning difficulties will have been seen by all members of staff. The information may be passed on but there is no guarantee. It is advisable to speak to each of your child's teachers, or to write a note to the effect that your child's file contains information that they might find helpful in understanding the nature of his learning difficulties. I am a little wary about the teachers who say that they would rather make their own observations and come to their own conclusions rather than be prejudiced by what others have discovered in the past. Very valuable time might be lost and situations handled inappropriately.

Getting the balance right between taking an active interest in your child's education, thus ensuring that he is being taught appropriately, and becoming a 'fussy parent' whom the school will avoid at all costs is a delicate business, but one that must be worked at for the sake of your child's future. If at all possible, try to develop a relationship with your child's school in which you are pulling in the same direction. There must be give and take on both sides. Try not to be confrontational when something goes wrong. Give the school a chance to explain their side of the situation. (However, if you are not satisfied with what they have to say, a little righteous indignation wouldn't go amiss.)

WHY SUCH AN EMOTIVE PROBLEM ?

Parents, teachers and other professionals can tend to become rather emotional when discussing dyslexia. Blame is apportioned to 'poor teaching', 'poor parenting', 'heredity' and so on. Teachers become defensive, parents feel guilty and children become confused, demoralized, withdrawn or disruptive.

None of this is helpful nor is it conducive to survival.

It is very important to start from the 'NOW'. What is the problem *right now?*

If it's unfinished or misunderstood homework, tackle that problem. If it's the fifth pair of plimsolls to be lost this term, then that problem takes priority. Tackle one problem at a time, otherwise the whole situation becomes overwhelming and everyone gives up.

CHAPTER 2

FUSSY MOTHERS

I thought it might be helpful to include a section on 'fussy mothers' for two reasons. The first is that most mothers of dyslexics that I have met have said at some time: "Am I just being fussy/neurotic/over-protective/expecting too much?''. If they haven't said it themselves then it is very likely that someone has said it of them. The second reason is that a few teachers might have a peep inside this book, and might find it useful to know what possibly makes a mother 'fussy'.

There's no denying that there are fussy mothers — I've been one — and as a teacher I have had to deal with some. However, I don't think many mothers are born 'fussy'. There are reasons for their so-called fussiness, and if they can understand why they become emotional about their dyslexic's schooling, and if teachers are also aware of the reasons, then with luck (and a little rational thought and discussion) something positive and constructive can come out of the fussiness.

WHAT CAUSES THE 'FUSSY MOTHER' ?

I think there are a number of factors, although not all of them apply at the same time, nor are they applicable to all mothers. They appear to be:-

> ANXIETY
> FRUSTRATION
> ANGER
> GUILT
> DISTRESS

1. ANXIETY over:
   a. her dyslexic's lack of school progress
   b. the discrepancy between apparent 'brightness' and actual performance
   c. history repeating itself (i.e. mother's or father's failure at school)
   d. her dyslexic's school phobia
   e. her dyslexic's failure to mix socially

All this can lead to over-protectiveness. A sense of proportion may be lost, and small issues or problems (e.g. teasing in the playground) may take on a disproportionate significance.

2. FRUSTRATION because of:-

a. teachers' apparent lack of concern
b. lack of information, both about the nature of her child's problem, and also about what the school is doing to remedy the situation
c. the feeling that her child is just a number, and not a person in his own right
d. feelings of utter helplessness

3. ANGER with:-
   a. school for apparently not taking action
   b. herself for letting the situation drift (''I knew there was a problem two years ago — I shouldn't have let myself be fobbed off'')
   c. her child for inconsistencies in behaviour and skills (''if he can build a 4-foot model of the Eiffel Tower out of spaghetti why can't he keep his bedroom tidy, or take a telephone message?'')
   d. herself for getting angry

4. GUILT that:-
   a. she has not done anything about the situation sooner
   b. the learning difficulty was probably inherited
   c. she isn't able to help her child at home (e.g. paired reading usually ends in tears)

5. DISTRESS over:-
   a. it being a lifelong problem
   b. what the future may hold in store
   c. not knowing if she's done the right thing

A SCHOOL'S RESPONSE

(The following suggestions are for any teachers reading this chapter.)
   When confronted by a 'fussy mother' I think it important to ask:-

   ''Why is she being fussy?''
   ''Am I doing anything that exacerbates the situation?''
   ''Am I handling the situation appropriately?''

Very often the school is fully aware of the dyslexic's difficulties and is doing everything in its power to help. However, parents are not always aware of this and so accuse the school of indifference or lack of expertise. It is so important that there is an ongoing dialogue between parents and school. This can be time-consuming and exasperating at times, but it is essential if the well-being of the pupil is to be assured.

There must be give and take on both sides. Schools must be prepared to listen to parents — parents really do know their children best; but parents must be realistic — just because a child has been diagnosed as dyslexic it does not mean that a special needs teacher can perform a miracle overnight. Remediating a dyslexic, even for the most experienced dyslexia teacher, is a long, uphill struggle.

A counselling approach with a 'fussy mother' should contain the following elements:-

    a. a sympathetic ear
    b. an interest in the pupil as a person
    c. information regarding the nature of the problem, both educational and social
    d. reassurance of normality
    e. ACTION

Depending on what is appropriate, ACTION may take the form of a teacher-assessment, a visit by a special needs teacher, referral to an educational psychologist, or all three — one may lead to another. Under the terms of the 1981 Education Act a parent can ask for a multi-disciplinary assessment if they are concerned about their child's education. (For more information, refer to the excellent book by Chasty and Friel — *Children with Special Needs.*)

When the assessment has taken place the results should be discussed with both parents. This is an important part of counselling, as appropriate expectations can be discussed. Parents often ask if they are expecting too much, or not enough, of their children. It is at this point that it can be explained whether their child is working at an appropriate level or not.

In addition to discussing educational difficulties, it is equally important to explain the wider implications of dyslexia. That is, the organizational and short-term memory problems. Frequently, parents are unaware that an inability to tie shoe-laces, to take a message, to follow a series of instructions, or to remember that Tuesday comes before Thursday is all part of the syndrome. Dyslexics can be very infuriating people to live with. It is problems with these skills that often give rise to accusations of the child not concentrating or of his being stupid. The danger is that, if you tell a child often enough that he is stupid, he will believe it.

The maxim that the Dyslexia Institute works to is: IF CHILDREN CAN'T LEARN THE WAY WE TEACH, WE MUST TEACH THEM THE WAY THAT THEY CAN LEARN. I would hope that all teachers could take this as their own motto.

WHAT ABOUT DADS?

The more I come into contact with dyslexics and their parents, the more I am aware of the important part dads play in the success (or otherwise) of any remedial programme. It is not the day-to-day active involvement, such as listening to the dyslexic read or helping with homework that is most important. Rather, it is a dad's attitude to the whole issue of dyslexia that seems to be crucial.

I don't know how popular I am going to make myself with the following observations, but I feel strongly that dads should take a moment to reflect on whether the stance they take is helping or hindering their dyslexic's development, both educationally and emotionally.

Dads seem to fall into a number of groups. This is not a definitive list and, obviously, some dads exhibit a mixture of these characteristics, but this is a starting point for reflection.

Dad 1. He takes no interest or can't see that there is a problem. He may comment "There's nothing wrong with him. He's just lazy/stupid/careless. You just make him work harder."

Dad 2. The chip-on-the-shoulder syndrome — "What's all the fuss about? Leave the boy alone. School did nothing for me, but look at me now. I've got my own business with a turnover of £X million."

Dad 3. This is the dad who may have had difficulties himself and can appreciate what his dyslexic is experiencing. He doesn't want history to repeat itself and does all he can to be supportive and encouraging — "I know there's a problem. I can see you're working hard, son, and I'll give you whatever help I can."

I don't think it's necessary to point out which is the most constructive stance to take. Dad 3 does so much to help ensure that his dyslexic doesn't lose heart. We all need to know that someone believes in us and accepts us for what we are. The dyslexic needs constant reassurance that this is so. Mums are nearly always understanding and supportive, and I'm afraid dyslexics rather take this for granted (in the same way that they take for granted tea on the table and clean socks in the morning). However, to have a male figure (dad, uncle, grandfather) believe in you, whether the dyslexic is a girl or boy, appears to be particularly significant if the maximum benefit is to be derived from any extra help given at school or in a dyslexia unit.

24

CHAPTER 3

WHAT DO YOU TELL YOUR DYSLEXIC?

It is very easy to talk over a child as if he is not there. It can be very confusing for him to catch snippets of conversation about 'specific learning difficulties, assessments, psychologists, special needs teachers'. However, I have often witnessed a positive and dramatic effect on a pupil when it is explained to him that he is not stupid and that we do not think he is lazy or not trying, but that there are reasons for his difficulties in learning to read and spell, and that they are not his fault.

A DIFFERENT WAY OF LEARNING

When the problems and reasons are fully explained it is often as if a great weight has been lifted from the child (or adult). I explain to pupils that they tend to learn things in a different way, so they need to be taught in a different way.

NO SHORT CUTS

I stress that they cannot use their dyslexia as an excuse — to be told that you are dyslexic simply means that you must work much harder than your neighbour. There are no short cuts. They will often say that it is not fair, and I explain that often life seems not to be fair but that they have just got to get on with it. It is a tremendous advantage for me to be able to tell them that I am dyslexic and still make awful mistakes, but that it is important to learn to laugh at them and to develop strategies to compensate. (I don't always own up to driving down one-way streets the wrong way!)

THE 'KNIFE-IN-THE-STOMACH SLOWLY TWISTING' SYNDROME

Explaining to your dyslexic the reasons for his difficulties is not always plain sailing. I remember trying to cheer Jonathan up on one occasion when he was about eight. He was very down about school and said that he was no good at anything. I tried to reassure him that he was good at lots of things and that we knew he was trying his best. I added that it was not his fault that he found things difficult but that he had inherited his learning

25

difficulties from me. This made him very angry and he blamed me for all his misfortunes. I call this the 'knife-in-the-stomach slowly twisting' syndrome. It lasted for about two years and it still upsets me to think about how hard school was for him at that time. He knew in his heart that he wasn't stupid, but he wasn't old enough to be philosophical about the many frustrations he had to experience.

MAINTAIN A POSITIVE ATMOSPHERE

It is at times like these that it is so important to maintain a very positive atmosphere at home. Comments such as 'I know it's tough but you will get there', and 'please help me with changing the fuse/putting up this shelf/mending the radio (or whatever is your dyslexic's particular skill), as you are the only one who can do it', should be commonplace. Letting him overhear your telling the neighbours, relations or the milkman about how clever he is at .... (whatever it is) is also a good ploy. Hearing comments like this over a prolonged period of time will have a positive influence on his self-confidence and feeling of self-worth.

HOME SHOULD BE A HAVEN

Home should be a haven where he doesn't have to feel a failure. He has enough of that at school. It can be very difficult if there are brothers and sisters who do not experience learning difficulties; comparisons are inevitable, but every effort must be made not to say anything within your dyslexic's hearing. Grandparents, aunts, uncles and the neighbours will have to be persuaded not to pass comments either.

MANIPULATE THE SITUATION

Hopefully, there will be some area where your dyslexic can succeed where his brother or sister can't. You might think it appropriate to manipulate the situation so that siblings don't always have the opportunity to compete. I don't know if Katharine realized that I wouldn't let her take up horse-riding as I thought she might prove a better rider than Jonathan (the cat is out of the bag now!). Fortunately, she was involved in a number of other hobbies so I could use the excuse that she wouldn't have time.

CHAPTER 4

ORGANIZATION AND THE DYSLEXIC

THE HEART OF THE PROBLEM

At the heart of a dyslexic's problems is an organizational difficulty. Most people appreciate that a dyslexic has difficulty organizing sounds and symbols into their correct sequence for reading and spelling, but it is often not realized that the dyslexic's untied shoelaces, incorrectly buttoned-up shirt, untidy bedroom, and difficulty with pronouncing words like *preliminary* or *statistics* are at least partly due to his dyslexia. I have often observed parents and teachers being very understanding, supportive and encouraging where problems with reading and spelling are concerned, but becoming cross and impatient if a book has been forgotten or games kit has been left at home because the dyslexic thought Thursday was Tuesday.

However, a word of warning: dyslexia is a possible explanation for poor organizational skills, not an excuse. The quickest way to raise the hackles of a teacher is for a pupil to say, ''I've forgotten my homework/plimsolls/violin because I'm dyslexic''. Please brainwash your child into never using dyslexia as an excuse. What are needed are strategies for compensating for these difficulties.

A POOR SENSE OF TIME

One of the first learning difficulties Jonathan manifested was a poor sense of time. It wasn't that he had difficulty in learning to tell the time, in fact he learned at a younger age than his non-dyslexic brother, but rather that he had difficulty with the concept of time. For example, he would not know which meal he had just eaten and which meal came next; knowing that it was 8.00 p.m., he would be surprised that the craft shop was closed; he would say 'today' when he meant 'tomorrow' or 'yesterday'. Learning the order of the days of the week and the months of the year can prove to be very taxing for many dyslexics. Even if the sequences can be learned, appropriate concepts do not always develop at the same rate e.g. it may have to be pointed out that most children don't go to school on Saturday or Sunday, that Bonfire Night is in November, that the summer holidays stretch across part of July and August, and so on. However, these skills can be mastered if appropriate help and support is given over a sustained period of time.

Here are some suggestions that are worth trying. Some worked for Jonathan and some I have used with various pupils. First, try to identify the specific problems your dyslexic experiences and then select a few strategies to slip into your daily routine. Do be discreet, don't try everything all at once, and do be patient. These suggestions take time to work.

TELLING THE TIME

1. If learning to tell the time is a problem I do recommend that somewhere in the house (the kitchen is often a good place) there is an analogue clock, and preferably one with Arabic numbers. Digital watches are very popular, but it is important that a child develops the ability to understand time expressed in different ways e.g. 1.40 p.m., 20 to 2, even 13.40 hrs. This is easier to demonstrate on an ordinary clock.

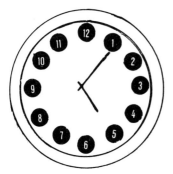

5.05 p.m.
five past five
17.05
five minutes past five o'clock

28

2. If you are asked, "What time is *Blue Peter* on?", say the time, "5 past 5", and then draw a clock showing the time (it doesn't have to be a work of art). Then leave your dyslexic to match your drawing to the kitchen clock. This helps with learning to tell the time in a meaningful way.

3. An extension of this idea can be used with an older dyslexic who experiences difficulties with telling the time, but who needs to be able to do so, in order to be punctual for an appointment. For example, if he has to go to his violin lesson halfway through the lunch break at 12.45 p.m. the drawing of a clock face can be supplied and kept in a pocket for easy reference.

4. Encourage your dyslexic to refer to the programme page of the newspaper or *Radio Times* to look up the time of his favourite programmes.

DAYS OF THE WEEK

1. Problems with the days of the week can be tackled in a number of ways. First, it is essential to have some kind of calendar in the kitchen (or in the room that is used before school in the morning). A wipe-clean board with the days of the week clearly marked or a Boots family calendar with a column for each member of the family to write their own reminders is ideal. This needs to be filled in over the weekend, preferably. For some years I used to do this after lunch on a Sunday before everyone left the table. We all discussed the coming week and what had to be remembered e.g. games bag on Tuesday, recorder on Wednesday, dentist on Friday etc. Drawings can be used instead of words. The aim is that eventually everyone takes responsibility for writing in their own reminders (remember, you are trying to make your dyslexic independent).

Every morning the day's reminders must be looked at before school so that the appropriate equipment can be taken and appointments can be kept. The system is not infallible, but it does help.

2. Allow the week's newspapers to accumulate around the house, and then ask your dyslexic to fetch 'today's'. He will have to check the top of each one to ensure that he has the right one

3. Make a point of referring to what happened *yesterday* or what is going to happen *tomorrow*.

MONTHS OF THE YEAR

One of the easiest ways to learn the order of the months of the year and to develop concepts connected with the passing of time is the daily use of a YEAR WALL PLANNER.

It can be used to demonstrate the answers to questions such as, ''how long is it until my birthday/Christmas/summer holiday'', or ''does October come before September?''.

YEAR WALL PLANNER

	JAN	FEB	MAR	APR	MAY	JUN	JUL	AUG	SEP	OCT	NOV	DEC
Mon				1			1			1		
Tues	1			2			2			2		
Wed	2			3	1		3	1		3		
Thur	3			4	2		4	2		4	1	
Fri	4	1	1	5	3		5	3		5	2	
Sat	5	2	2	6	4	1	6	4	1	6	3	1
Sun	6	3	3	7	5	2	7	5	2	7	4	2
Mon	7	4	4	8	6	3	8	6	3	8	5	3
Tues	8	5	5	9	7	4	9	7	4	9	6	4
Wed	9	6	6	10	8	5	10	8	5	10	7	5
Thur	10	7	7	11	9	6	11	9	6	11	8	6
Fri	11	8	8	12	10	7	12	10	7	12	9	7
Sat	12	9	9	13	11	8	13	11	8	13	10	8

It should be used to record all forthcoming events for the family. (A fine-nibbed pen is needed for this as there is not much room!) Birthdays and other special occasions can be high-lighted with a fluorescent pen. It is then an easy job to count the weeks until the SPECIAL DAY arrives. Our wall planner is kept in the kitchen and gives our busy family life some semblance of order, or at least it allows us to predict the times when the children need taking to parties at the opposite ends of the county on the same day! Jonathan struggled to learn the months of the year by heart, but he achieved it in the end by constant reference to the planner. Now he uses it to check how many weeks are left in the month, and whether his allowance will last that long! A logical progression from this is the use of a diary or better still, a personal organizer. I have a jumbo-sized organizer containing A5 size plastic wallets into which I slip all the little pieces of paper, receipts, and bills that I might otherwise lose. I find it invaluable: my life would grind to a halt if I lost it!

You can try teaching the 'Thirty days hath September ... ' rhyme; girls often pick this up, but the boys have more difficulty. Another system is to use the knuckles of the hands-

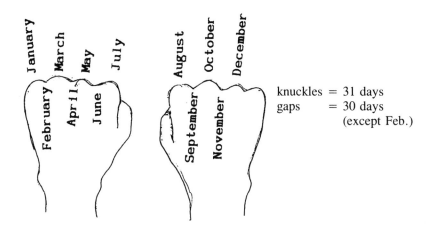

knuckles = 31 days
gaps = 30 days
(except Feb.)

Point of interest — does your dyslexic omit May and October when sequencing the months of the year? (These are the fifth and ten months.) Dyslexics find it very difficult to hold five items in their memory (or even three of four) and this may be the reason why these particular months get forgotten.

Knowledge of the SEASONS may not be quite as important, but a thick red line can be drawn through the wall planner to separate the months.
—Roughly speaking the months are grouped:-

SPRING	March, April, May
SUMMER	June, July, August
AUTUMN	September, October, November
WINTER	December, January, February

MEMORY

Dyslexics are notorious for their poor memories. They can read a word at the top of the page, but by the time they see it again further down the page they have forgotten it. They read the word 'friend' on the blackboard but write down 'frend'. Trying to learn their times tables is a nightmare. They lose things; they forget peoples' names; they can't remember instructions; they miss appointments. Strangely, they can remember every detail of the holiday they had four years ago!

IF IT'S LOSABLE, HE'LL LOSE IT

If it is losable, he'll almost certainly lose it, or leave it behind, or put it somewhere and be unable to remember where. If you can accept this fact and come to terms with it, much frustration and loss of temper can be avoided. If he doesn't lose it, you count that as a bonus. However, I did not say that you must be resigned to the situation: there are strategies to be employed. The most obvious and easiest one is to NAME EVERYTHING that goes out of the house. This might result in some items being returned by kind friends and neighbours. However, consistent organizational skills are required. The easiest method I have found is to have a honey jar (it's useful to have a see-through container as the contents act as a reminder) containing name tapes, sewing cotton, a threaded needle and an indelible marker pen readily available — mine sits on top of the 'fridge. Articles need to be named as soon as they are bought. If you leave it until you have time it will not be done; it will leave the house, probably never to be seen again.

'HE'S GOT TO LEARN' or
'ANYTHING FOR A QUIET LIFE'

Implementing the following strategy depends on your own philosophy and ground rules. There are times when it is necessary for children to learn from their own mistakes, just as there are times when you may wish to opt for the 'quiet life'. The contents of the P.E. bag seem to be the items that are lost most often. My strategy is to have spares of everything bought very cheaply at the school swap shop. (If your school doesn't have one, start one now; other parents will bless you for it.) You will not know that anything is missing from the bag until two minutes before it's time to leave for school or when your dyslexic informs you that he has a detention/hasn't played football for two weeks/had to do P.E. in his underpants because he didn't have the right kit. Being able to supply the correct item instantly can avoid the trauma of a distressed child going to school knowing that he's going to get into trouble yet again. This strategy needs to be employed sparingly as you don't want him to think you will always be there to bail him out. As stated earlier, your aim should be to make him self-sufficient.

VISUALIZATION AND TALKING ALOUD

When looking for a lost item it can be useful to retrace one's steps either physically or in the imagination, whilst at the same time giving a running commentary ALOUD e.g. "I went into the kitchen to get a biscuit, and then the 'phone rang and I went into the hall to answer it — oh yes, I know where I put the scissors, they're by the phone." Saying things aloud seems to aid recall.

TAKING MESSAGES

Taking messages is usually quite a challenge for the dyslexic. A dyslexic's memory will always be unreliable, but there are strategies that can be learned. One of the most powerful is to repeat the information aloud. If you want your dyslexic to take a message, first ensure that he is looking at you and paying attention (we gain so much information from the speaker's body language), say the message clearly and then ask him to repeat it back to you. It may be necessary to repeat this procedure a couple of times before he is confident. It might be possible for him to visualise the instructions: this can be particularly successful if sent to the shops to buy three items e.g. a loaf of bread, a pot of cream and a tin of baked beans. This could be visualised as baked beans on toast, topped with a whirl of whipped cream. (Test yourself later to see if you can remember what was needed at the shops: I bet you have no difficulty in remembering the three items.)

In order to take a telephone message it is essential that there is an ample supply of pencils and scrap paper by the 'phone. Your dyslexic is unlikely

33

to remember the message in his head, or if he does, he is unlikely to tell you that he has a message. He must be encouraged to write down key words, or at least the initial letters relating to the message. Failing that, he could draw the message. He might be able to take the 'phone number of the caller, but this is quite an art. I have difficulty in doing this myself, but over the years I have developed the following strategy — as soon as the caller has said three digits I cut in and repeat them to him; I then let him say the next three and then repeat those. When the whole number has been given I repeat the number back to the caller and ask if it is correct. As it is unlikely that your dyslexic will remember to tell you that he has a message it is advisable to ask him if anyone has 'phoned while you have been out.

Tony Buzan has written widely on memory techniques: his ideas usually rely on linking ideas together or associating what needs to be remembered with what is already remembered. You can read more about this in 'Use Your Head'.

PERSONAL ORGANIZATION

Some dyslexics have difficulty dressing themselves or, at least, putting on items in the right order. For a number of years I put Jonathan's clothes out for him the night before, piling them in the order in which they were needed. This saved untold hassle in the morning, when I was trying to get everyone ready for school. Now, I try to ensure that his socks, pants, T-shirts etc. are in separate drawers so that he has to take just one item from each.

I tried having a laundry bag hanging on his bedroom door but this didn't work as I forgot to empty it! Having one central basket for the whole family seems to work much better, although Jonathan still has to be reminded to scoop the clothes from his floor and deposit them. However, he does have just one corner of his room for the pile so perhaps before he leaves home he will get the hang of the system.

Most dyslexics take much longer than their peers to learn how to tie their shoelaces: what a blessing velcro fastenings are!

In an attempt not to lose too many clothes when Jonathan went on school holidays I would sellotape a clothes list inside the lid of his suitcase. He could then check that he had the right number of items when he packed to come home. This worked fairly well, although the seven pairs of socks brought home weren't necessarily his and there would often be extra items that he had found lying around. The list would be used when originally packing and Jonathan became so familiar with this routine that now he is the most efficient packer of the family. A plastic bag labelled 'Dirty Clothes' ensured that at least some of these were packed separately from the clean ones and acted as a reminder that he was meant to change his socks occasionally!

Although Jonathan might dispute this, I tried not to nag too much by asking if he had washed his face/brushed his hair/cleaned his teeth, etc. Instead, I established the house rule that he had to kiss me goodbye before he went to school. In this way I could secrete a hairbrush behind my back in case it were needed, I could smell the toothpaste, and I could see if the Marmite had been removed from his face. If all was well, I did not need to say anything except "have a good day". If your dyslexic's poor organizational skills frustrate you beyond reason try to tackle them one at a time and come to a compromise that will be mutually acceptable to everyone concerned. Give and take will be needed, but having agreed to the house rules, make sure that they are enforced (well, most of the time!).

THE BEDROOM QUESTION

Oh, for a family of bird-watchers! Nicholas, our non-dyslexic son is a keen ornithologist, and the untidiness in his room is limited to the odd reference book not put back on his shelf and a pile of RSPB magazines by his bedside. He's not wonderful about hanging up his clothes, but at least they are in a pile on his chair.

Jonathan's room, however, is quite another story. To say that it resembles the aftermath of a hurricane is an understatement. He is a born inventor and scavenger. (Remember the Wombles?) He likes making things: not, I hasten to add, neat Lego buildings or Meccano cars, but large, Heath Robinson-type contraptions involving metres of string, wire, batteries, flashing lights, loudspeakers, (or whatever else he has managed to find in a skip).

There was the time that he asked us to come to see the spider's web that he had made. It was intricately woven and filled the whole room. It was attached to the four walls and was about three feet above the floor. We admired the engineering feat and said that we didn't mind the whole room being taken over, but that we drew the line at Nicholas being the fly. Nicholas (who was about six at the time) was sitting on the bed at the centre of the web very firmly tied up!

House rules have to be set and compromises have to be made. Perhaps the biggest compromise I made was when Jonathan was about thirteen. Once again we were summoned to his room and told to stand by the door. On Jonathan's desk (which resembled more a work-bench) was a plastic dinosaur that had been acquired free with one of the breakfast cereals. Jonathan had made it look like a dragon: at the touch of a button real flames shot out of the dragon's mouth! Apparently, he had scavenged for the remains of fireworks after Bonfire Night and had organized a controlled explosion. He had taken great care over the organization and I hadn't the heart to put a stop to his experiments. However, the compromise was that Jonathan was given a fire extinguisher for Christmas with the clear instructions that it had to be kept in a very prominent place and not hidden under all the mess on his floor.

The noisiest invention involved wiring up his door handle to a tape recorder and four speakers: by opening the door a circuit was completed and music blared out at about a hundred and twenty decibels. He managed to get in and out of his room by the use of a pass key which broke the circuit.

There are times when it is best to close your dyslexic's bedroom door and pretend the horrendous mess you have just seen inside doesn't really exist! My non-dyslexic daughter, who also lets her room become pretty untidy (although not in the same league as Jonathan) commented on one occasion when instructed to tidy-up, 'This is my room and I like it like this!'. She had a point. We all need a bolt-hole, a place where we can unwind and blot out the day if necessary. If that includes having the room

37

in a terrible mess to make it feel homely, then who am I to suggest that it should be cleared up? On one occasion when I asked Jonathan if his friends kept their rooms in such a mess, he replied that some of them had very tidy rooms but they were SO BORING. (I think he meant the rooms, not the friends!)

Most of the time I can come to terms with the mess (I'm quite untidy myself) but there are times when I think enough is enough and strategies come into play. Jonathan has come to accept the house rule that I will tolerate so much and then the big tidy-up has to happen. He can do this for himself now, but it took some years of training. We all have our own methods of spring-cleaning but this is mine:

1. Empty containers are needed. I never throw anything away. Margarine pots, ice-cream tubs, honey jars with screw lids and biscuit tins are invaluable. In addition, two large cardboard boxes are required.

2. Jonathan would sit on the bed and direct the proceedings; I would sit on the floor. I would pick up whatever was nearest and ask, ''Treasure or rubbish?''. (As nearly everything looked like rubbish I found it difficult to tell.) The 'treasures' would be put into one box and the rubbish into the second. I would work my way around the floor until everything was clear. I usually allowed him to keep the top of the odd cupboard or desk in a mess so that the room didn't look too boring.

3. The rubbish was disposed of and the 'treasures' were sorted. This is when the empty containers were put to good use. I encouraged Jonathan to put all the string in one tin, the wire in another, and so on. The honey jars were ideal for small objects and allowed the contents to be identified without removing the lid.

4. The containers were then labelled and stored on shelves, in cupboards and under the bed.

5. Eventually, Jonathan appreciated that this kind of organization saved time in the long run as it was easier to find things. In due course, he learned to carry out the procedure for himself. That is not to say that his room is always kept tidy — far from it; but he has the required strategies for doing something about it. The present house rule is that he has three warnings when his room becomes a health risk (he is allergic to household dust); if he doesn't sort his room out I move in and do it when he is not around, and I may well throw away numerous 'treasures'. He rarely needs a third warning!

Postscript — Jonathan has bought a Morris Minor to 'do-up' which actually means stripping it down completely; he has just asked me for empty shoe boxes and small plastic bags to store all the nuts and bolts in. I hasten to add that this is happening in our garage and not in his bedroom — I'm not that tolerant.

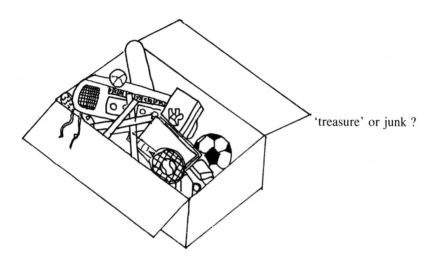

'treasure' or junk ?

CHAPTER 5

HELPING WITH READING

'GOVERNMENT' HEALTH WARNING!

Trying to teach your own child can seriously damage your health, or, if not your health, cause severely frayed tempers and a nasty hiccup in the child/parent relationship. I am not advocating 'teaching' your child (although if your child wants you to and you can manage it, then that's a bonus), rather, I hope to show ways in which you can create an atmosphere in which your child can learn. This can be achieved through subversively inculcating better organizational skills, encouraging memory strategies and above all by displaying your belief and confidence in your child's abilities, even when the going gets tough — and it can get very tough indeed.

At an early age Jonathan made it very clear that he wanted me to be 'mum'. After a stressful day at school trying to keep up with his classmates he needed home to be a refuge, a place where he could relax and be himself. He did not want to be put into a situation where he might fail. As a teacher, I found this very frustrating: I felt that there was so much that I could teach him. However, it was essential that I respected his wishes. This did not mean that I had to sit back and do nothing, but it did mean that I had to be quite subtle in my approach.

THE MORE YOU DO, THE BETTER YOU GET

Learning to read is like learning to walk and talk : the more you do the better you get. The problem for the parents of a dyslexic is how to persuade him to do something that he finds difficult, frustrating and possibly boring.

HOW DO WE LEARN TO READ?

The mechanisms involved in learning to read are not fully understood, but we know that various strategies come into play. It is not simply a matter of recognising individual words or blending individual letters into words. There is more to it. Here are some of the important factors:

(a) THE TITLE — if the title is 'The Rescue' it would be reasonable to expect the story to be about someone or something rescuing someone or something. Children often omit the title when they begin reading a new book. This is unfortunate as they are often overlooking a useful piece of information.

(b) PICTURES — if the first page has a picture of a dog stuck in a large hole, the chances are that this is what the story is about. Introducing picture books to children at a very early age is an important pre-reading experience. They should be encouraged to describe what they can see in each picture, and possibly make up a story of their own. It gives the parent, or whoever is sharing the book with them, the opportunity to introduce them to words that they do not know e.g. "That's a mechanical digger. Do you know what it's for?", or "That's a robin. Sometimes we call him robin red-breast. Why do you think we call him that?"

(c) PREDICTION — ask "What do you think will happen next?". This line of questioning can begin with picture books e.g. there is washing on the line, the wind is blowing hard, ask "What is going to happen to the washing?" When reading to your dyslexic, stop at an exciting bit and ask "What do you think will happen next?". With luck, this kind of discreet training should help him develop the habit of hazarding a guess when he is reading e.g. *"Tom stood on the edge of the cliff and looked over. The edge began to give way and he plunged into the sea."* He might not know the word *plunged*. If he is following the sense of the story he might substitute the word *fell*. This is fine as it shows that he is understanding what he is reading and can replace a tricky word with a simpler word that makes sense. However, he may spot that the substitute word is not correct as it begins with the an 'f' and not a 'p' and he might then be able to self-correct.

(d) INITIAL LETTER and GENERAL CONFIGURATION — Combining his ability to predict what is probably coming next and his knowledge of initial blends i.e. *pl*, and the length and shape of the word, he might be able to make an educated guess as to what the word should be.

(e) A FEELING FOR THE LANGUAGE — An ability to predict is also developed by reading to your dyslexic. It helps him to become familiar with the way we put English together to express ideas (grammar). This should help him to predict a word that is grammatically correct.

(f) READING TO YOUR DYSLEXIC — The most important thing that a parent can do to help his dyslexic is to read to him. This will probably need to be done for longer than for the non-dyslexic. (I was still reading exercises onto tape for Jonathan when he was sixteen). Obviously, if a parent experiences difficulties with reading this is not so easily done. But in the early stages it doesn't matter if the reading is not error-free; your non-reading dyslexic will not be able to spot the mistakes. Later on you may want to enlist the help of grandparents, the baby-sitter, or any other willing reader. Reading to your child, whether dyslexic or not will also help to establish the idea (which is obvious to us, but very often not to children) that all the squiggles and black lines on the page represent the sounds that come out of our mouths. This can be quite a revelation for some children. The blocks of lines on the page (words) have spaces between them, but much of what comes out of our mouths is in one continuous flow. In fact, we encourage children not to leave spaces between the words when they read aloud as it makes them sound like a Dalek! All this can be quite confusing for some children.

However, getting back to my original statement, it all needs lots of practice. But how do you get him to co-operate?

(g) LITTLE BUT OFTEN — It has been found that, if a poor reader can read with a parent (or anyone else who is a proficient reader) for ten minutes a day, five days a week for eight weeks, he can improve his reading age by six months or more. It's the 'little but often' that is vital. It's like training for a marathon. Running five miles a day four times a week is much better preparation than running twenty miles once a week.

(h) PARENTS AND TEACHERS UNITE! — Very often, a child will be more willing to do his ten minutes a day if it is at the direction of his teacher. If you can work together with his teacher you are more likely to get your dyslexic's co-operation. A record book or sheet is a useful way for a parent and teacher to communicate. The teacher can indicate how much she would like read and the parent can add comments as to how long the reading took, if there were any particular problems e.g. "still has difficulty reading *said*", and any general comment as to how the session went, "he raced through this", "he enjoyed the story", "he found it boring/too difficult" etc.

(i) PAIRED/SHARED READING — Various terminology is used to describe reading-practice approaches. There tend to be quite a lot of fads and fashions in the educational world and the jargon used seems to be added to daily. It can be rather confusing. However, here are some approaches that you could try. What suits one parent and child will not necessarily suit another. It is necessary to experiment and adapt to find a formula that suits your particular circumstances. There isn't a right way and a wrong way, although there are some general do's and don'ts.

(j) THE DOs and DON'Ts — A reading session at home with mum, dad or the babysitter should be considered as *reading practice* and not a reading lesson. Leave the teaching side to another time. The whole point of reading a book is to get information and/or enjoyment from the session. Nothing will kill that enjoyment more than for the child to be stopped in the middle of a word to 'sound-it-out', or to be asked, "You could read that word at the top of the page, why can't you read it now?" If he makes a mistake or gets stuck, just give him the word, making sure he repeats it after you. A mental note can be made to let the teacher know about words that are causing a problem, or you can reinforce them at a later date.

DO choose a time for reading that is mutually agreeable; not during his favourite television programme.

DO let him choose a book that HE wants to read (unless he has a class reader that needs to be practised).

DO make it a cosy affair (e.g. sit together on a couch).

DO tell him a word he can't read, but don't jump in too quickly; give him a chance to have a go.

DO praise him a lot (go over the top! 'that was fabulous/terri-fic/super/great/you are getting better').

DO read together regularly.

DON'T stop in the middle of a sentence to get him to 'build a word'.

DON'T get irritable with him when he gets stuck on a word that he read correctly on the previous page.

DON'T let a younger brother or sister comment, "Can't you read that? It's easy!" If possible, keep siblings out of the room during the reading session.

DO award yourself a medal (or a double gin) if you can manage all of the *dos and don'ts!*

DON'T feel guilty if you can't.

Method 1 — SIMULTANEOUS READING

This method requires you to read aloud with your child e.g. you both read 'Simon went for a walk by the river' at the same time. It can be helpful if one of you runs your finger along the top of the line so that you are both reading the same word at the same time. The idea is that you are giving your child total support during the reading session. You are also modelling how the reading should be done i.e. you use appropriate intonation, and pause at punctuation marks. You need to aim at being a split second behind your child so that he is having a go at the reading and not merely repeating what you have said. If he hesitates you can give him the word, but get him to repeat the word before he carries on. Don't let him struggle with a word for more than five seconds. It takes a little practice to get into the swing of this method, but it can relieve the pressure greatly for an insecure reader and make the story far more enjoyable as continuity is maintained. When the reader becomes more confident, he can signal that he wants to read on his own (still aloud). The pre-arranged signal may be a tap on the table or his elbow in your ribs. When he signals that he wants to continue on his own, you say 'well done', or something similar, and let him continue until he gets stuck; you then tell him the word and continue reading with him until he signals again that he wants to read on his own.

Method 2 — MODELLING

This can be an effective approach with something that is quite difficult for the reader. Some children insist on choosing a book that is too difficult, but they can be helped to cope by using this method. First read a page to your child. Then read the page together using method one. Finally, let your child read the page on his own. If it is something that particularly interests him you will be amazed at how well he manages. Obviously, he has memorized much of the page due to the repetition, but this is not a problem; it is all part of the reading process.

Method 3 — TESTING PARENTS' COMPREHENSION!

This is a method for use with the moderately proficient reader who needs more practice but who is very reluctant to do any. The parent gets on with a routine job e.g. peeling the potatoes, ironing, cleaning the shoes. The reader reads his book aloud and every page or so stops to ask the parent questions on the story or article (if it is a magazine or newspaper). If the reader becomes stuck he can ask for help (without having to have the parent peering over his shoulder all the time); if something doesn't make sense because of misreading or a disregard for punctuation, the parent can say, "Hang on a minute; can you read that again? I didn't quite understand that bit." In order for the reader to ask questions, he will have to understand what he has read and so his own comprehension will improve.

COLOURED OVERLAYS

There has been a great deal of interest in the use of colour-tinted spectacles. It is thought by the Irlen Institute that *scotopic sensitivity syndrome* (sensitivity to specific wavelengths of light that cause eye-strain and various visual distortions) can be helped by the use of tinted lenses. It is an area that is keenly debated by the experts with some supporting the use of the glasses and others having serious reservations. However, it is quite fun to experiment with coloured plastic overlays. Sheets with a matt finish can be obtained from the Irlen Institute, or a more restricted selection of colours can be bought at some stationery shops (these tend to be quite shiny so there can be problems with reflected light). Some of my pupils find these overlays quite helpful when they are reading. They comment that the print is clearer and that letters don't jump about. It is difficult to judge to what extent it is the novelty aspect or to what extent the coloured filters do make reading more comfortable, but if it means that your dyslexic is more willing to read or can keep going for longer, I don't think it matters.

TAPED STORIES

I am a great advocate of taped stories, either homemade or commercially produced. There is a rich variety of stories available. Cassettes can be bought at record shops, often from book shops, and from department stores. Alternatively, they can be borrowed from the record section of public lending libraries. Sometimes the tapes are straight readings of a story, sometimes the stories have been dramatised. Very often they are read by well-known actors.

The advantages of listening to taped stories are numerous, but some of the most important ones are that:-

1. the listener can become familiar with a wealth of literature appropriate to his age and ability.
2. the listener can become familiar with an increasing sophistication of English usage.
3. the listener can continue to extend his vocabulary.
4. hopefully, the listener will develop a love of stories.
5. the listener is introduced to new horizons (non-fiction is available as well — we have a splendid tape on the climbing of Mount Everest).
6. it's fun!

Some people feel that listening to story tapes is somehow cheating, that it will stop dyslexics from trying to read, or that there is little value to be gained. In my experience, all these accusations are far from the truth. Jonathan was given a boxed set of 'The Lord of the Rings' by J.R.R. Tolkien when he was thirteen. He listened to all the tapes so often that he nearly wore them out. Because he knew the story so well, he then went on to read the three-volume book for himself and subsequently used the land of *Middle Earth* as inspiration for a most imaginative computer project for GCSE. As he has continued to listen to stories of ever-increasing complexity, so his vocabulary has kept pace with his development in other areas. As he very rarely reads books for pleasure, I am sure this would not have happened if he had not been kept supplied with tapes.

45

Cassettes are often sold with an accompanying book so that the script can be followed whilst listening to the tape. Unless the tape is being used for study purposes, I am not too convinced that this is always advisable. It can inhibit the imagination because the listener is often preoccupied with trying not to lose his place and concentrating on when to turn the page. I would rather the listener were lying on his bed conjuring up pictures in his imagination whilst listening to the narrative.

I have been asked by parents, "But how do you get them to sit still long enough to listen to a story?". That was achieved easily in our household: our children (non-dyslexics enjoy the experience just as much as dyslexics) listened to the tapes in bed just before they went to sleep. All I had to remember was to go round their rooms to turn the tape recorders off before I went to bed. In fact, Katharine at nineteen will still listen to a taped story if she can't get to sleep (Sherlock Holmes or Jeffrey Archer stories are ideal, she says) and we have just bought Nicholas recordings of the two Shakespearian plays he will be studying for 'A' level.

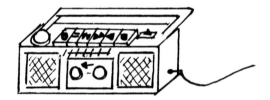

CHAPTER 6

HELPING WITH SPELLING

THE PROBLEM

The problem with spelling is that you are either right or wrong: you can't get away with an educated guess as you can with reading. Spelling involves remembering a visual pattern. Dyslexics often have inefficient visual memories. They may remember the letters that are needed to spell a word, but will not remember the order in which to write the letters e.g. *flet* for *felt*. It should be possible to sort out this kind of problem by listening to the order in which the letters occur e.g. *f-e-l-t*. However, this can have its limitations, as so many words cannot be spelled the way they sound e.g. *sed* for *said*. To make spelling even more complicated, the same sound can be represented by different letter combinations e.g. in theory, the word *kite* could be spelled *kyte* or *kight*. Those who have difficulty with spelling need to develop a number of strategies to supplement their unreliable memory.

A MULTI-SENSORY APPROACH

If the visual memory is poor then other senses must be used to make up for any deficiencies. By this I mean that *touching, saying* and *listening,* as well as *looking,* must be used if spellings are to be remembered. If you ask someone how to spell a word they might say, "Hang on a minute, let me write it down". They may well want to see that it 'looks right', but they will probably know if they have spelled it correctly by the time they have finished writing it, because it 'felt right'. They know how to spell the word because they are used to writing it.

Some words are remembered by pronouncing them using a *spelling language* e.g. *Wed-nes-day.* This is using the sense of feeling, but in the mouth this time. It also uses the sense of hearing.

The DREADED SPELLING TEST

The following ideas can be used for learning both English and foreign words.

(a) First, look through the list to see if any words are already known. If there are a few, this will ease the learning load and the task may not seem so daunting.

(b) If the list is a formidable one (more than ten words) it might be best to tackle just a few words each day, if time permits.

(c) Sometimes, in a test situation, children are expected to spell correctly just 50% or 75% of the words in the list for it to be considered a pass mark. If this is the case, and if some of the words are proving very difficult to learn, it might be better to concentrate on learning sufficient to reach the pass mark and to forget about the others!

(d) Look for words within words e.g. he*ar*d, re*presen*tative, *Marseille* — '*Eating Mars Bars in Marseille makes you ill.*'

(e) Highlight, with a fluorescent pen, the tricky bits — *au*tomatic, r*h*ythm, d*oe*s.

(f) Make up a mnemonic (memory trick). The sillier the better
e.g. O U Little Darling for c*OULD*, w*OULD* and sh*OULD*
    ICI is an eff*ICI*ent company.

(g) Write the words out in large (30–50 cm) lower case letters, either print script or joined up. The word is said aloud, then the letters are named as they are traced over with the index finger of the preferred hand, then the word is said again. This is repeated until the word can be written from memory.

(h) Write the word IN THE AIR moving the whole arm, or link the hands together and use both arms together. Say the word, name the letters, say the word.

(i) One-third fill a seed tray (no holes in the bottom) with salt. Using the index finger, write the word in the salt, say the word, name the letters, say the word.

(j) Place a piece of coloured paper (red or black is best) on a tray. Write the word with a GLUE STICK. Sprinkle the word with SALT. Shake off the excess salt. See the word appear. When it is dry it can be used for textured finger tracing. Variations of this are endless — dried pasta or rice could be used in place of salt.

(k) Make the word in PLAY DOUGH, PLASTICINE or real BREAD DOUGH (this could be baked and the word eaten — anything is worth a try!)

(l) Use a WATER PISTOL to write the word on a brick wall. (I can't imagine any dyslexic refusing to learn their spellings using this method — even sixteen-year-olds.)

(m) LOOK — COVER — WRITE — CHECK. Look at the word, identify the tricky bit, use (d), (e) or (f) as a memory aid, cover the word, write it from memory, check to see if it is correct. This procedure should be repeated at least three times, even if the first attempt was right. Try writing the word with closed eyes. This seems a bit tame after (l) but is the method often used in schools. A class of thirty children with water pistols might be a bit over the top!

DIFFERENT KINDS OF DICTIONARIES

I am very keen on the use of dictionaries. I think their use should begin very early on. However, for the dyslexic, dictionaries are not easy to use and the selection of the right dictionary for the right situation is essential.

THE ALPHABET

A pre-requisite for using a dictionary is being able to sequence the alphabet. This can be learned with the aid of plastic or wooden letters (magnetic ones for the fridge door are useful as you can supervise an alphabet session whilst you are peeling the potatoes.) Many dyslexics find using uppercase letters easier initially as the shapes are more distinctive and fewer letter confusions are made. (However, never write words in block capitals for your dyslexic to copy.) Singing the alphabet is a great help. I use the tune below.

Initially, it can be helpful if the dyslexic is given a copy of the alphabet to reproduce with the letters. The alphabet can be divided into piles of five or six letters, and then each group can be sequenced. This makes the task far less formidable. I have known quite young dyslexics master the alphabet in two or three weeks.

PERSONAL SPELLING DICTIONARIES

Many schools have class word books where high-frequency or topic-based words are listed. Sometimes pupils are supplied with their own word book. Words that they use often in free writing, but which they can't spell, can be added as required. An excellent spelling dictionary for teenagers has been compiled by Eileen Stirling. It contains the words most often required, and mis-spelled by teenagers. Each page has room for additional words to be entered. It has a plastic cover for durability and fits easily into a blazer pocket or the side pocket of a school bag. If your dyslexic does not have a personal word book, then an indexed notebook, such as the type used for addresses, is ideal.

PUBLISHED SPELLING DICTIONARIES

As the title implies, these contain just spellings; definitions are not included. These can be ideal if it is just the spelling that is required. Dyslexics often become quite confused and put off by the mass of words in a conventional dictionary, and they can have difficulty working through the definition to find the word they are seeking. Base words with suffixes added are included, so there are no worries about whether to drop the 'e' or double the last letter. Some include place names and rivers. The *Oxford Mini-Dictionary of Spelling* will fit into a blazer pocket.

PHONETIC DICTIONARIES

The Pergamon Dictionary of Perfect Spelling is an excellent example of a phonetically arranged dictionary. Very often, a dyslexic can't find the word he wants because he is looking under the wrong initial letter. He won't find *photo* in the 'f' section of a conventional dictionary, but he will find the spelling *foto* in this dictionary with the correct spelling of *photo* next to it. Incorrect words are printed in red and the correct versions are printed in black. Regrettably, this dictionary is now out of print but it is well worth searching out a secondhand copy.

AURALLY CODED ENGLISH SPELLING DICTIONARY
(ACE for short)

Looking a word up in this dictionary involves quite a different procedure from most (if not all) other dictionaries. Initially, an index is used; a page number is given by cross-referencing the first vowel sound and the first sound of the word. It is quite difficult to explain how the dictionary is used without your having a copy in front of you. However, once it has been demonstrated, it is quite easy to use. Many special needs teachers use the ACE dictionary, so if your dyslexic has never seen one in use, he could ask at school for a demonstration.

ELECTRONIC DICTIONARIES

These vary in size ranging from that of a pocket calculator to that of a large pencil box. The word display is similar to a calculator. To check a spelling it is necessary to type in an approximation of the word. The computer indicates whether the word is correct. If it is not, it supplies the correct spelling or, if it is not sure which word was being attempted, it gives a number of possibilities. It is necessary to be a reasonable reader (probably with a reading age of ten years or over) as the correct word must be recognised when a list of possibilities is presented. Some models offer definitions, contain a Thesaurus, or have games. The novelty of using an electronic gadget can be highly motivating and some dyslexics will be more inclined to check spellings using such a computer rather than a conventional dictionary. It is certainly much quicker. I think they are excellent, although rather expensive (between £60 and £100). Before splashing out on such a purchase I would recommend borrowing one for a day or two so that your dyslexic can try it out. If his spelling is too bizarre it would not be of much help. These comments apply also to the use of a spell-check on a word processor.

CONVENTIONAL DICTIONARIES

Although I am an enthusiastic user of all the different kinds of dictionaries mentioned above, I still think it important that dyslexics learn to use a conventional dictionary as well. Once a reasonable reading age is reached this is a viable proposition if an appropriate publication is available, and providing the dyslexic is shown how to find his way around the dictionary efficiently and quickly.

The choice of dictionary is a personal one, but a few points should be kept in mind:

1. Are the target words well defined? Are they printed in bolder print? Do they extend into the margin?
2. Are the definitions relatively easy to understand? Are the target words put into sentences as a means of illustrating their meaning? (I have one rather old dictionary in which the definitions are more difficult to understand than the target words!)
3. Is the method for explaining pronunciation easy to follow? (My favourite dictionary rewrites words phonetically e.g. *foto-sintha-sis* for *photosynthesis*. (Bold print is used to indicate where in the word the stress falls.)
4. Is the size of print appropriate for the user?
5. Is the colour of the paper comfortable to look at? Some dictionaries have very black words on very white paper and this can cause eye strain or visual distortions for some dyslexics.
6. Is the size of the dictionary appropriate? If it is too large it will not be carried around in a school bag and so will not be available when it is needed. Sometimes it is advisable to have a smallish dictionary for school and a larger, more detailed edition at home.

My favourite dictionary is the *Heinemann English Dictionary*. I still think that it is the easiest to use for a dyslexic. However, many new dictionaries have been published since then, so it is very important to shop around when choosing one. It can be a good idea to visit a large bookshop or W.H.Smiths and try looking up the same word in a selection of dictionaries to see which feels the most comfortable.

INCREASING EFFICIENCY

It is possible to increase the speed at which a word can be found quite considerably once a few facts are learned:

If a dictionary is opened up in the middle the letter M will be found; if the first half of the dictionary is divided in half again the letter D will be found; and if the second half of the dictionary is divided it will be opened at the letter S. Thus the four quartiles of the dictionary will contain the following letters:-

    1st quartile: ABCD
    2nd quartile: EFGHIJKLM
    3rd quartile: NOPQR
    4th quartile: STUVWXYZ

Children love putting this to the test and impressing their friends with the boast, "I can turn to the 's'-es in one go."
I teach the mnemonic, 'All Elephants Nibble Sausages' to remember the first letter of each quartile.

Children also need to know that the word in the top left hand corner of the page is the first word of that page and the word in the top right hand corner is the last word on that page. Thus, if the word printed at the top left is *fellow* and they are looking for the word *fabulous*, they must turn *back* a page or two as 'a' comes *before* 'e'. Likewise, if the word in the top right of the page is *fetch* and they are looking for *fight*, they must turn on a page or two as 'i' comes *after* 'e'. It goes without saying that they need a sound knowledge of the alphabet and must appreciate the concept of 'before' and 'after'.

CHAPTER 7

HELPING WITH MATHS

Research suggests that 60%–70% of dyslexics have difficulties of some sort with maths. They may well become good mathematicians eventually, but in the early stages, when arithmetic is required, they often do quite poorly. The reasons for this are directly related to the underlying problems dyslexics experience when learning to read and spell — problems with short-term memory, sequencing and orientation.

If your dyslexic is struggling in maths. you need to ask a few questions in order to understand what is causing the problems. When the precise difficulties are identified it is easier to work out what help and support is needed.

POSSIBLE PROBLEMS

1. Muddling similar shapes: + and x, 6 and 9.
2. Difficulties with adding on; he may have to go back to 1 each time (in the same way that he has to go back to 'A' each time he gets stuck when saying the alphabet) e.g. if adding 5 and 2 he may have to say 1,2,3,4,5.....6,7.
3. Problems with counting backwards, thus experiencing difficulties with subtraction.
4. Difficulties learning tables and formulae; or, having learned his tables, difficulties with jumping about e.g. having to start at the beginning of the table to work out 6x7.
5. Difficulties with remembering the direction to work in. Reading and writing go from left to right, but sums sometimes go from right to left as well as left to right, or even top to bottom, bottom to top and even diagonally. It can be very confusing!

   This directional problem can also be seen with the child who adds 6 and 7 and says 13, but writes 31!
6. Setting work out correctly can be a problem
   e.g. 63 + 142 may be written down as 63 +

   $$\begin{array}{r} 63\,+ \\ \underline{142} \\ \underline{772} \end{array}$$

The addition of the individual numbers is correct but the answer is wrong. This problem occurs not only when making a sum from

54

information contained in a problem but also when copying sums from the blackboard.

7. Problems with short-term memory may lead him to forget what he was doing halfway through a sum, so having started off subtracting he may end up adding. This also happens when saying tables: he may 'dry up' in the middle and ask 'where am I up to?'

8. Difficulties with remembering a sequence of operations needed to work out a sum, as in long division.

9. Difficulties with reading the problem. He may be able to do the sum, but cannot read all of the words that the sum is wrapped up in.

10. Difficulties with labels e.g. x, *times, multiply, product, square* and *power* can all mean the same.

Many dyslexics who experience difficulties with arithmetic understand the mathematical concepts involved; they just make errors in the recording or workings out. Sometimes they get behind because they don't know their tables or cannot add up in their head, resulting in their working very slowly. For a small minority, the problem is much greater, as they do not have well developed concepts of numbers e.g. they may not understand that you cannot change direction when subtracting: $7-9$ is not the same as $9-7$.

WHAT TO DO

If your dyslexic says he cannot do his maths., sit with him while he has a go, and ask him to say aloud what he is doing. It might then become evident where the problems lie. If at all possible try to lead your dyslexic to spot the mistakes for himself. If that doesn't work, try to show him where he is going wrong so that he can put it right. Try not to do the sum for him. Sometimes it is better to get an older sibling or the boy next door to help because mathematical jargon changes every ten years or so and it is difficult to keep up-to-date. Showing him how you did it when you were at school might add to the confusion.

If the nature of the maths. is such that you cannot help, ask at school for guidance.

LEARNING TABLES

Learning tables is often the biggest mathematical problem for dyslexics. It is worth trying tapes of tables that are set to pop music. The use of rhythm is often a great aid to memory. I am also a great advocate of the table square illustrated overleaf.

To work out 7x6, run the left index finger across the page starting at number 7 in the left hand column whilst running the right index finger down the page from number 6 until the fingers meet. You should land on 42.

1	2	3	4	5	6	7	8	9	10	11	12
2	4	6	8	10	12	14	16	18	20	22	24
3	6	9	12	15	18	21	24	27	30	33	36
4	8	12	16	20	24	28	32	36	40	44	48
5	10	15	20	25	30	35	40	45	50	55	60
6	12	18	24	30	36	42	48	54	60	66	72
7	14	21	28	35	42	49	56	63	70	77	84
8	16	24	32	40	48	56	64	72	80	88	96
9	18	27	36	45	54	63	72	81	90	99	108
10	20	30	40	50	60	70	80	90	100	110	120
11	22	33	44	55	66	77	88	99	110	121	132
12	24	36	48	60	72	84	96	108	120	132	144
	2	3	4	5	6	7	8	9	10	11	12

The fingers can be used to work out the 9 times table. Have your hands side-by-side, palm side uppermost. If the sum is 4x9, bend the 4th finger of the left hand; that leaves 3 fingers on the left of the bent finger and 6 to the right (thumbs are included). Thus the answer is 36.

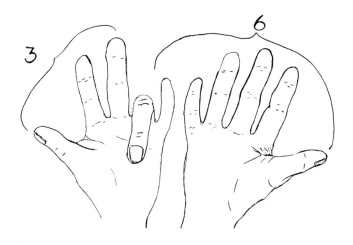

Dyslexics often have to use concrete aids for longer than many of their classmates. These don't have to be expensive maths. aids: often pencils, buttons or tiddlywinks will do (or if you are into bribery, Smarties are highly motivating, as they can be eaten when the homework is finished!).

Ordinary drinking straws are useful when trying to explain the carrying figure in subtraction. I cut the straws into four and then bundle them into tens, securing them with the little elastic bands supplied with jampot covers. When a 'ten' has to be transferred to the units column it is possible to demonstrate how one 'ten' is made up of ten units by removing the elastic band.

I helped one pupil overcome her phobia with times-tables by baking fairy cakes. Whilst greasing and filling the individual sections we counted how many cakes we would make. I then led her on to see how we could use our tables to work out the total without having to count every one. This was 'real' maths., and she quickly learned that knowing her tables could be useful.

There are a number of very good books available that go into more detail about the difficulties some children have with maths., and they suggest numerous strategies and games. In particular I would recommend *Maths for the Dyslexic* by Anne Henderson.

CHAPTER 8

STUDY SKILLS

It is becoming increasingly popular in schools to teach Study Skills and I applaud this move. There are some pupils who are extremely efficient; their work is beautifully presented; they understand instructions; they give in assignments on time and they do not leave revision to the last minute. However, for many pupils (not only the dyslexic ones), this is not the situation and they need specific help with learning how to study more efficiently.

Your dyslexic needs to get into the habit of saying, 'Am I doing this as efficiently as I can? Am I wasting time? If I have been efficient, can I use the same work approach in a different situation?'

As I explain in the chapter on *Homework,* it is an advantage if:-

1. there is a regular time for working
2. there is a regular place for working
3. the *what, when, how* are understood

Kid gloves need to be used in making any of the following suggestions to your dyslexic, but one or two of them might come in useful if the going gets tough and your dyslexic asks you for help.

HAVING THE RIGHT EQUIPMENT

Dyslexics often get into trouble at school for arriving at a lesson without the required equipment. It's easy to waste time looking for pens, pencils etc. This checklist might be useful for the beginning of a new term. (It actually needs looking at before the first day of term and before the shops close!) The precise items required will depend on the age of your child and the subjects he is studying.

Checklist: writing pens (try different types)
           cartridges
           coloured pens and pencils
           lead pencils
           pencil sharpener
           rubber
           ruler
           geometry set
           scissors

hole punch
ring reinforcers
files, folders and dividers
A4 paper
plastic folders
highlighter pens
overhead projector pens (non-permanent)
glue
sellotape.

PRIVATE STUDY

It is very easy for a dyslexic to waste time when studying on his own either at school or at home; he may be required to work on an assignment or to revise for a test or an examination. If he has ensured that he has all the equipment he needs and knows what he has to do he should get off to a good start, but it may be difficult for him to switch off from what he would really like to be doing in order to concentrate on the job in hand. It might be helpful if he thinks of the work period like a session in a multi-gym: he wouldn't try to work-out on the most difficult piece of equipment straight away; he would do a warm-up first, then exercise specific muscles, and would finish with a general cool-down. His brain needs to be treated in a similar way: first he needs to review the work he has already done just to get his mind tuned-in; then he needs to concentrate on the difficult part of the work being attempted; he should then finish by reviewing the work he has done — proof-reading for errors, ensuring that he hasn't omitted any important details, or checking how much he has remembered if he is revising for a test. A work schedule might look like this:

Routine: 5-10 minutes: revise previous work
          20-40 minutes: tackle new or difficult work
           5-10 minutes: go over notes, check what has been learned.

If he finds working for an hour difficult, he should have a break every twenty to thirty minutes; he could walk round the room, have a drink, but should NOT switch the television on!

TAKING DICTATION

It might be because I find this skill difficult myself, but I think this is probably one of the most difficult tasks that can be given to a dyslexic. It requires so many skills: firstly, the sentence or phrase has to be held in

59

short-term memory (most dyslexics have a very poor short-term memory), secondly, the spellings of words have to be puzzled out (whilst concentrating on breaking a word into syllables, or trying various combinations of letters, the rest of the sentence is often forgotten); thirdly, handwriting and fine motor control have to be attended to (many dyslexics just cannot write very quickly); fourthly, capital letters, apostrophes and other punctuation marks have to be remembered; lastly, everything has to be done at speed (it may not seem fast to many of the other pupils, but it will seem fast to the dyslexic).

What can be done to support the dyslexic?

(i) Encourage him to 'have a go' but suggest that he leaves gaps for the words he can't spell and copy from a friend later.

(ii) Show him how to use abbreviations for common words.

(iii) Ask a friend to place a piece of plain paper and carbon paper under his work in order to make a copy. (Permission would be required from his teacher first.)

(iv) Copy from his neighbour, either during the lesson or later. (Permission should be sought from his teacher and his neighbour first.)

(v) Photocopy a friend's notes to keep in a file or copy-up at a future date.

(vi) Ask the teacher to supply a copy of his/her notes.

(vii) Tape record the lesson and transcribe later. (I'm not too keen on this method, as editing a 40-minute lesson is a skilful job, but I know it has worked for some pupils.)

If at all possible, let the teacher know that dictation is a problem for your dyslexic. However, I know that many dyslexics prefer that attention is not drawn to this particular difficulty, so tread very carefully when trying to find a solution.

MAKING AND TAKING NOTES

This is a very close second to TAKING DICTATION in the level of difficulty for a dyslexic.

There are two kinds of note-taking: making notes from a book, and taking notes from a speaker.

MAKING NOTES FROM A BOOK

The first skill your dyslexic has to grasp is that of spotting key words and main ideas. For example:-

On the 14th October 1066, the French Duke William and his army fought against the English King Harold and his army at Senlac Hill, where the village of Battle now stands

The main idea is the battle between Duke William and King Harold. The key words are underlined below.

On the 14th October 1066 the French Duke William and his army fought against the English King Harold and his army at Senlac Hill where the village of Battle now stands

Notes on this sentence could be made like this:

1066   Duke William defeats King Harold   Senlac Hill (Battle)

These very brief notes should be sufficient to trigger the memory and the fact that William was French and Harold was English would probably be remembered without including it in the notes. Alternatively, this information could be recorded as a cartoon.

There are two ways to practise picking out key words:-

1. If a photocopy of the work can be obtained, demonstrate how to scan through the writing, marking the key words with a highlighter pen: fluorescent yellow is a great favourite. This can be done first and then the notes can be made by concentrating on the highlighted words. This cuts down the reading load considerably and helps the dyslexic focus on the main points.

2. If a photocopy is not available, obtain a clear plastic wallet into which can be slipped the page to be studied, and a waterbased pen designed for using with an overhead projector. The writing is scanned, and key words underlined, proceeding as (1). As long as the pen is waterbased, the ink can be cleaned off the plastic. Remove the book first as it is easy to wipe the ink onto the page if it extends beyond the wallet.

I have found that when students use highlighter and overhead projector pens the task never seems so onerous.

(If the mechanics of reading is slowing your dyslexic down too much, you can offer to tape-record the work so that he can play the recording and follow the script at the same time, stopping the tape to allow him to mark key words.)

These key words can be written onto box-file cards and used for memory triggers the night before an examination. This system of note-taking is equally as effective for eight-year-olds as for university students.

NOTE-TAKING FROM A SPEAKER

This can prove to be very difficult and is akin to taking dictation. All the problems associated with dictation apply to taking notes from a speaker and are made even more complicated because the note-taker must select what to write down. As with taking notes from a book, the strategy is to be aware of main ideas and key words. If your dyslexic has had experience of taking notes from books he will find it easier to pick out what is relevant.

If he is lucky the speaker will say, "Today I am going to talk about ....". That is the main idea and the title for the notes. It must be written down quickly. If your dyslexic is really lucky the speaker will carry on to say, "I will be considering three main areas connected with this topic: they are 1......., 2......., 3.......". These are important subheadings and your dyslexic should then either divide his page into three and write down these headings for each section, or should write the headings at the top of three separate pages. The speaker may jump from one idea to another, but the notes can be kept in an orderly fashion.

Your dyslexic needs to practise writing just key words, no *ands*, or *buts*. Hopefully, he will develop his own system of abbreviations, arrows, equals signs etc. to help speed things up.

The important thing (and the strategy that requires the most self-discipline) is to write up the notes as soon as possible after the talk whilst the subject is still fresh in his mind; if he leaves it too long he may not remember what all his abbreviations mean.

I would hope that he is not put into the situation of taking notes like this too often. If he is, he might have to employ some of the strategies suggested for taking dictation.

WRITING ESSAYS

Writing an essay can prove a major problem for a dyslexic; it requires good organizational skills — not a dyslexic's strong point. A dyslexic often knows what he wants to say; he knows the facts or he has the imagination, but he just can't organize his thoughts sufficiently to write a clear and well-constructed piece of work that does him justice. However, you can show your dyslexic various planning techniques that will make the task far more manageable.

THE 6-POINT PLAN

I was shown this planning strategy whilst training with the Dyslexia Institute, and I have used it with both seven- and seventeen-year-olds with equal success. It is ideal both for imaginative stories of the adventure type e.g. *Holiday Adventure, Small but Brave, Man's Best Friend,* and also for an empathy-style essay based on fact e.g. *Imagine you were living in Pudding Lane at the time of the Fire of London.* It can comprise just six sentences or run to a number of pages. A younger child can illustrate each section, or draw the pictures first for you to write the captions at his dictation.

For the planning stage, fold a piece of paper into six sections, and write a heading at the top of each box. Key words can be written under each heading before the essay is tackled.

1. The People	2. The Place	3. Something Begins to Happen
4. The Exciting/ Dramatic Bit	5. Things Sort Themselves Out	6. The Ending

1. PEOPLE

This section introduces the character/s, who may be a child, an adult or an animal; the story can be written in the first or third person. A description of the character's appearance, personality, age, job, hobbies, etc. can be included. If there is more than one character their relationship can be explained. Here are some examples:

    a. My name is David. I am ten years old. My favourite hobby is rock climbing.

    b. Tom was very small for his age and the other children picked on him.

    c. Ben was a scruffy looking dog but he was very friendly.

    d. My name is Kate. I worked at a bakery next door to my home.

2. THE PLACE

The story needs to be set in a location. Information about the weather, time of year, scenery, etc. can be included.

    a. I went on holiday to the seaside. It was very hot. There was a good cliff face to climb.

b. He went for a walk by the river. It was a windy day.
c. Ben didn't have a home, and rummaged round the dustbins in people's back yards looking for scraps to eat.
d. The houses were very close together and I could hang out of my bedroom window and talk to my friend who lived in the house opposite. It was very smelly as people threw all their rubbish into the gutter.

3. SOMETHING BEGINS TO HAPPEN
The scene has now been set and the tension begins to build up.

a. Mum told me not to climb the cliff by the beach because it wasn't safe, but I didn't take any notice. Halfway up the cliff the rock under my left foot crumbled and I began to fall!
b. He could see a little girl standing by the edge of the river. Suddenly, a big gust of wind blew her into the river. She couldn't swim!
c. He saw some children playing hide-and-seek. One child climbed into an old freezer on the dump and closed the lid.
d. I don't know what woke me up but I was suddenly aware that I could smell burning.

4. THE EXCITING/DRAMATIC BIT
This is the climax of the story; it will probably make reference to the title.

a. I grabbed at a tree growing out of the cliff. Everyone shouted at me to hang on, as the rescue helicopter was on its way.
b. Without thinking, Tom kicked off his shoes, jumped into the river and swam to the little girl.
c. Ben stood by the freezer and barked and barked until someone came to see what all the fuss was about.
d. I shouted, "Fire! Fire!", grabbed my baby brother, climbed out of my bedroom window and dropped to the street below.

5. THINGS SORT THEMSELVES OUT
The story cannot be left in the middle of a climax: solutions must be found or problems sorted out.

a. The helicopter hovered overhead and lowered a rope ladder for me to climb.
b. Tom heaved with all his might and managed to drag the girl to the river bank where the onlookers pulled her ashore.
c. Someone opened the freezer lid and was amazed to find a small child cowering in the corner.
d. All the wooden houses burned to the ground. I was so scared.

6. THE CONCLUSION/TIE UP LOOSE ENDS

This can be quite short. It can refer to the title, a moral can be drawn or a pithy comment can be made.

  a. It was quite an adventure, but not one I would like to repeat. Parents DO know best!
  b. Tom was hailed a hero. He was small but brave.
  c. Ben was called the cleverest dog in the street and he never went hungry again.
  d. London was rebuilt; this time, the houses were spaced much further apart.

The first draft of an essay, written to this plan, can be quite brief, with just the main idea for each paragraph written down. These ideas can be developed and written about in greater detail for the second draft.

DESCRIPTIVE WRITING

A second planning technique that was passed on to me is very useful if a descriptive piece of writing is required e.g. *A Walk By a River, A Visit to a Castle, The Funfair*. This involves imagining that you have a camera and using your senses.

For example, you arrive at the funfair and before you enter the gates have a general look around: what can you see, hear, smell? How does it make you feel? Key words could include:-

  SEE top of helter-skelter, big-wheel, roller-coaster
  HEAR screams, music, 'roll-up, roll-up'
  SMELL hotdogs, motor oil, toffee apples
  FEEL excited, nervous

A general description would make up the first paragraph.
You then put the camera to your eye and focus on one area and describe that in detail:-

  SEE helter-skelter, red and black stripes, pile of mats, people queuing
  HEAR child asking, 'can I have a go?'
  FEEL 'I'd like a go'.

Not all the senses need to be included in each paragraph.
The final paragraph requires looking through a zoom lens at one very small detail

  SEE child sitting at top, look of excitement mixed with fear, holding on tight, looking over edge
  HEAR squeal of child as he pushes off and lets go

FEEL perhaps I'll miss that one out!

No reference need be made to the camera; the shape of the essay will be a wide overview of the scene, a more detailed description of one area and then very detailed observations of something quite small.

SPIDER DIAGRAM

The spider diagram is a very popular method of planning an essay and can be used successfully by both children and adults. It can be used for any subject where an essay has to be written. A large sheet of scrap paper is needed. Any number of legs can be included. First, draw a spider —

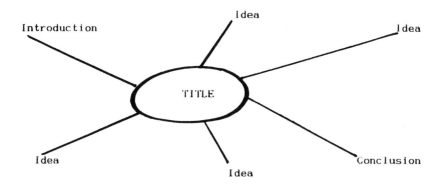

The essay title should be written in the body of the spider. This must be referred to constantly to ensure that the planning is keeping to the point and that nothing is being omitted.

Each leg represents a paragraph: key words should be listed under paragraph headings. The first paragraph will be the introduction and the last paragraph the conclusion. *Brain-storming* can take place and details can be jotted down under suitable headings as they come to mind. If details are written in the wrong place, they can be crossed out. When all the information needed for the essay has been recorded, the spider's legs can be numbered in the order for writing up. As each piece of information is included in the essay, it can be ticked off, thus ensuring that nothing is inadvertently omitted.

This planning technique can be used both for homework and also in an examination. In some instances, if a candidate runs out of time in an examination, but has written a plan on the paper, he may be given some marks for the preparation.

Using this technique can help alleviate feelings of panic in the dyslexic. It helps him to organize his thoughts, to write coherently, and to minimise the omission of important details. Pupils who tend to include too much information in one sentence, resulting in their losing the thread of what they are saying, need to be encouraged to take one key word at a time and to write one sentence about that, and then to take the next key word and to write the next sentence, and so on. When they have become proficient at simple sentences, they can be shown how to join sentences together, still keeping to one main idea per sentence, but with supporting detail.

WHO? WHAT? WHERE? etc

This is a favourite method for writing a history essay. The order of the paragraphs can be changed to suit the topic. Each paragraph can be just one sentence long or can be developed to a considerable length.

WHO did it?
WHAT did he do?
WHERE did he do it?
WHEN did he do it?
WHY did he do it?
WHICH way did he do it?
WHAT was the RESULT?

LEARNING WORK

One of the main characteristics of dyslexia is a poor short-term memory. It follows that learning information for a test is going to pose a problem. If this can be overcome and information can be learned and stored in long-term memory, there remains a second dyslexic problem — word-finding and memory retrieval (getting out of the memory what went in). I have somewhat over-simplified the idea of short-term and long-term memory: it is more complicated than this and there are some psychologists who feel that no clear distinction between different types of memory can be made. Perhaps it is sufficient to say that memory activities are a problem for dyslexics.

Dyslexics tend to absorb the general concepts of a subject and can tell you what things are for, but cannot always tell you what they are called. This results in their using terms such as 'thingummy' and 'what-d'you-call-it'. Learning spelling lists, times tables, history dates, lines of poetry, names of rivers etc. can prove at least an onerous task if not a nightmare.

It is very difficult for a dyslexic to improve his memory (I haven't had much success with mine!), but there are strategies that can be learned that will compensate for this weakness and help the dyslexic feel more in control.

Here are a few suggestions for learning work. It is not a definitive list, but it is a starting point and it may lead you to develop further strategies that will aid your dyslexic.

BE ACTIVE

The most important advice you can give your dyslexic is to be ACTIVE when trying to learn. Just reading something through is not sufficient. We have all had the experience of reading a page in a book or newspaper, then realising that nothing has sunk in, and so the page has to be read again. This is a common experience for the dyslexic; it is important that he find ways of stopping his mind from wandering.

If you can persuade your dyslexic to try some of these strategies, it will be important for him to ask himself these questions afterwards:-

1. Did that strategy help me to concentrate better?
2. Could I work for longer?
3. Have I remembered more than I usually manage?
4. Have I understood more?
5. Would it be useful if I used this strategy again?
6. Could I use this strategy for another subject?

Not every strategy works for everyone. It is very important that your dyslexic discovers what works for him. It may not be your ideal way of working: we are all individuals with our own learning style and this must be respected (providing it works!).

STRATEGY 1

a. Quickly read through what has to be learned to get a rough idea of the content.
b. Read through again, but slowly, listing the main ideas or key words.
c. Read through the key words.
d. Try to write the key words from memory.
e. Repeat (c) and (d) until sufficient is being remembered.

f. Later in the day, or the next day, see how many key words can be remembered.
g. Revise what has been forgotten.

The key words could be written on box-file index cards and used for last minute revision.

STRATEGY 2

(This is similar to STRATEGY 1.)
a. The dyslexic will need his own text books or photocopies of work to be learned.
b. Read through work quickly.
c. Read through work slowly, highlighting key words in a fluorescent pen.
d. Try to link key words together using a visual picture or a silly story. (Silly stories, especially if they are rude, are much easier to recall than dry facts!)
e. Try to write the key words from memory.

STRATEGY 3

Study skills books and educational psychologists reports often refer to a process of studying called SQ3R. This stands for:-

S *Survey* — get general impression of work (author, date of publication, chapter headings etc.)
Q *Question* — why are you reading the book or chapter?
what do you expect to find in it?
R *Read* — read quickly for overall impression
mark key words and ideas
R *Recall* — from memory, note everything you can remember
R *Review* — (at a later date) check what you have remembered and note what you have forgotten

There are two important conditions for successful learning:-

1. The work must be understood.
2. Constant revision is essential.

If a new topic is looked at just once, it is unlikely that more that 25% will be remembered. If it is looked at again the next day it is probable that as much as 50% will subsequently be remembered. If it is looked at again for a third day the percentage retained will increase markedly, and if it is reviewed a week later and then a month later, most of the information will be stored firmly in long-term memory.

If you would like to know more about memory and how it can be improved, read any of Tony Buzan's books, especially *Use Your Head* and *Use Your Memory*.

CHAPTER 9

HOMEWORK AND THE DYSLEXIC

This chapter could be subtitled 'Nervous Breakdown Time'. One of the greatest causes of stress in the homes of many dyslexics is the nightly homework session. Before any strategies are suggested for coping with this I think it important to consider why it is so stressful. When the cause of a problem is identified you are halfway to finding a solution.

WHY IS IT A PROBLEM?

1. *Many dyslexics are extremely tired when they get home from school* and the last thing they want to think about is home- work. They might just flop or they might appear somewhat hyperactive. However they may appear physically, their brains have usually had enough for the time being.

It is sometimes suggested that dyslexics have a short concentration span. This may be so, but for many I feel it is that they have had to concentrate so hard on EVERYTHING during the day that they run out of their day's quota of concentration earlier than their non-dyslexic classmates. Even quite minor occurrences during the day can sap their energy. For instance, a class may be told that Mr Jones is away and so after break they are not having P.E., but are to go to room 10 where Mrs Brown will be looking after them, and that they are to take a library book. This can set up all manner of stresses for a dyslexic. Firstly, he has to remember the instructions (remembering a series of instructions proves taxing for many dyslexics); next he has to find room 10 (he may not have been there before and being told to turn left after the gym is not much help if he doesn't know his left from his right!); lastly he has to take a library book (what does he do if he hasn't got one with him?). One would hope that he would tag along with someone who can cope with this organizational skill, but it is still likely to lead to a feeling of being not quite in control.

2. Very often *the required instructions or books are missing* (quite often both!). The instructions may have been given orally and instantly forgotten, or they may have been written on the blackboard for the class to copy down. Many dyslexics experience great difficulty in copying accurately and at speed from the blackboard. If they can't read what is written it is akin to a non-dyslexic trying to copy Chinese — it would probably be done symbol by symbol. This would be very laborious and time-consuming. The chances are that the bell would ring for the next lesson before the task was

71

completed. Remembering to take the correct books home needs good organizational skills — not a dyslexic's strong point. Some will cope with this by carrying all their books around with them at all times — quite a feat of strength!

3. Very often a dyslexic will say that *he doesn't understand what he has to do*. This may be connected to (2) because he hasn't copied the instructions completely; alternatively, it may be because he has misread the instructions. It is quite common for a dyslexic to omit a word, such as 'not', thus completely changing the sense of the question.

4. The problem may well arise due to *poor study skills*. He may not know how to plan an essay and so end up writing all his ideas in one paragraph of six lines when he has been told to write at least a page and a half. He may have to learn spellings, tables or a set of facts for a test and, having read the work through and realized that nothing has sunk in, may panic and say that he can't do it.

Before you can be in a position to support your dyslexic when he is doing his homework there are certain pieces of information you should have:

1. How long should the homework take?
2. The purpose of the homework?
3. When was the work set and when is it due in?

Your dyslexic may be able to supply the information, or you may need to talk to the teacher(s) concerned. Tread carefully with the second course of action: the older your dyslexic, the more he will object to your 'interfering'. A *Parents' Evening* may well be the appropriate occasion for gleaning information.

HOW LONG SHOULD IT TAKE?

The length of time the homework takes can be quite a problem. The chances are that any piece of homework will take your dyslexic longer than a non-dyslexic of the same ability. It will take him longer to organize himself; he will write more slowly; he may well be more tired. Some teachers will instruct the class to do what they can in half an hour. This sounds very reasonable, but many dyslexics are not prepared to hand in work that has taken them the designated length of time, because they know that it will be much shorter than that produced by their classmates, and some comment may be made about 'trying harder' or 'finishing the rest at break'. They will often prefer to stay up later, even if it does mean tears and frayed tempers.

With younger pupils it might be worth negotiating with the teacher so that only a proportion of the 20-word spelling list has to be learned, or that a list supplied by his learning support teacher (if he has one) be learned instead. If an essay has to be written, perhaps an essay plan can be made with one or two of the paragraphs written up and the remainder completed at the weekend.

With younger children, at least, communication with the teacher concerned is very important if there is a problem over homework. If the work is completed to an adequate standard there is no way a teacher can know that it has been produced through enormous effort. Most teachers would much rather know that there is a problem so that appropriate strategies can be worked out.

THE PURPOSE OF HOMEWORK

Knowing the purpose of the homework is essential as this will dictate how it is to be tackled. There are four main areas:-

  (i) completing work begun in class (at GCSE level this may include coursework and assignments)
 (ii) consolidation (i.e. practising something that has just been learned)
(iii) learning for a test
 (iv) investigative (e.g. 'find out all you can about the blue whale')

To avoid the panic of work being left to the last minute, the weekly planner mentioned previously needs to be used. If there is a set pattern to homework this needs to be entered on the planner. Use different coloured pens for 'work set' and 'work due in', e.g. if ten spellings are given on Monday to be tested on Friday, write 'spellings' in red on Monday (this will remind you to ask your dyslexic if he has brought the list home), and 'spelling test' on Friday. This will help you to get your dyslexic to pace himself so that a few words can be learned each night, or learned on a night when there isn't too much else going on.

THE IMPORTANCE OF A ROUTINE

To minimise the trauma of nightly homework a routine is essential. You need to negotiate with your dyslexic to come up with a formula that is thought to be reasonable by both of you (don't expect him to work when his favourite T.V. 'soap' is on). Having negotiated this, you need to be quite tough until the routine is established. The chances are that it won't be easy at first, but if you succeed you will have helped your dyslexic develop work habits that will probably last a life-time. (I am ever the optimist!)

Plan of action for when he gets home from school:-

1. Feed him. It is unlikely that your dyslexic will be able to get on with his work the minute he gets home. Let him have something to eat; a honey or Marmite sandwich will do him more good and keep him going longer than a bag of crisps. When my children were younger I would prepare a plate of sandwiches earlier in the day and leave them on the kitchen table so that everyone could help themselves when they got home. This meant that the routine could be maintained even if I was busy when they arrived. We had house-rules on the number of sandwiches they could eat so that they didn't spoil their appetite for the evening meal, and to ensure that there were some left for the last person in.

2. Let him watch television, kick a ball around, play on the computer — relax. Your dyslexic needs to unwind for a while; the day may have been stressful.

3. DON'T ASK "Have you had a good day? What have you done/learned?". If something good has happened he'll tell you, if it's been awful he doesn't want to talk about it, or at least not yet. Perhaps at bedtime everything will pour out and then you can commiserate and have a cuddle.

4. Decide, by discussion with your dyslexic, *when* homework is to be done. This may differ each day depending on swimming lessons, what's on television, the weekly shopping trip, how many hours of sunlight are left for playing outside etc., but, ideally, there should to be a weekly routine that needs modifying only occasionally. It will be a battle, but do try to stick to the routine. It will become established eventually. The occasional bribe might prove helpful on difficult days!

5. Decide, by discussion, *where* the homework is to be done. If it is possible to have a designated space that is reserved for homework, then this is ideal. It can have a strong psychological effect as it will be associated with work and so it will be easier to get started more quickly. (Dyslexics are expert at procrastinating!) It can be organized so that books, pens and pencils or whatever is needed on a regular basis can be to hand. It is very easy to waste time if equipment has to be looked for.

For some dyslexics, a bedroom might be the right place; for others this is too isolated and a corner of the kitchen is best, as it is easier to ask for help if there are people around.

Siblings may need splitting up. My own experience was that having three children in the same room doing their homework was a recipe for instant

74

disaster. They would interfere with each other or pass unhelpful comments such as, "Can't you do that? That's easy!". We were fortunate to be living in a four-bedroomed flat so they had their own rooms to which they went to do their homework. For two or three years, during a crucial stage of their education when they needed a good deal of support, I would spend a frantic hour or two going from room to room giving help. It is quite a juggling act trying to avoid jealousy between dyslexic and non-dyslexic siblings and the needs of all your children have to be kept in mind.

6. The area needs to be distraction-free. Comics, pieces of Lego or whatever else could be used as a diversion need to be nowhere in sight.

7. Music? Personally, I can work only in total silence, but my dyslexic is quite adamant that he can't work unless he has music playing at the most fearful volume. We gave way over this when he proved to us that he had thought it through very carefully. His argument went as follows:-

    a. It stopped his mind from wandering.
    b. He couldn't hear anything else that was happening in the flat so wasn't distracted.
    c. He only played music with which he was very familiar; he would stop to listen if it were something new. Consequently, he played tapes rather than the radio.
    d. It stopped him from becoming bored.

We were very sceptical, but as he revised for his GCSE's with the most awful noise emanating from his room and achieved 2 'A's, 3 'B's and 3 'C's at a first attempt (these included English Language and English Literature), I have subsequently reviewed my ideas!

I remain unconvinced that homework can be efficiently tackled with the television on, unless it is the most routine colouring exercise.

HOW MUCH HELP SHOULD YOU GIVE?

This is a very thorny question. There are a lot of 'IFS'.

1. IF he doesn't have a homework diary supply him with one.
2. IF he can't write the instructions from dictation quickly enough suggest that he copy from a friend at break, or ask his teacher to enter the details into the diary herself (this, of course, depends on his age).
3. IF he can't copy the instructions from the blackboard, do as above.
4. IF he forgets to to bring home the books he needs, put a sticker on his pencil case, or somewhere similar, saying REMEMBER HOME-WORK BOOKS.

5. IF none of this works, ensure that you have the telephone number of a non-dyslexic classmate who will have all the necessary information. (I have been known to take from dictation over the phone a whole maths. exercise because the necessary book was not brought home.)

Remember, you are trying to ensure that your dyslexic becomes an independent learner. Ultimately, he must take responsibility for his own learning. It can be done. Jonathan is often phoned by friends asking for homework details as everyone knows that he is the organized one!

6. IF he has the instructions and the books but says that he doesn't know what he has to do, ask him to read you the instructions or question. He may have misread some of the words, inserted or omitted vital words or ignored the punctuation and consequently made nonsense of what he was reading. By re-reading (with prompting from you if necessary) he may well say, "Oh, I see what I have to do; I don't need any help now."

7. IF 6 doesn't work, ensure that he understands the key words. See if he can put the instructions into his own words. If he can't, explain the question to him.

8. IF he has answered a similar question before, ask him what he did last time, or look at the examples in his book.

9. IF it is something that he has just learned, ask him to tell you how his teacher would do it.

10. IF none of these strategies are working, and tempers are becoming frayed, TELL HIM WHAT TO DO. But this is a last resort and you will need some discreet way of letting his teacher know that there is a problem.

11. IF he can't answer the question because his notes are inadequate, or unreadable there are two issues to tackle: first, how is he going to complete his work for tomorrow, and second, how is he going to avoid this situation in the future? It is to be hoped that this scenario is not taking place too late in the evening so that a friend with adequate notes can read them down the phone (have a tape recorder handy so that you can repeat them on to it). You may be able to find the information in your own reference books. Finally, he may have to ask for an extension and give the work in late. Depending on his age, you may have to write a letter to his teacher to this effect. To avoid this situation in the future see the chapter on *Study Skills*.

There are a number of ways to help your dyslexic with his homework without actually doing it for him.

76

USING A TAPE RECORDER

We have used a tape recorder with Jonathan from the age of eight right up to GCSE. Very often there is a fair bit of reading to do before the questions can be answered or the essay written. If the reading is not the prime object of the homework, then I think it is perfectly reasonable to record the reading for your dyslexic. This can relieve a great deal of pressure as often the dyslexic is so daunted by the mechanics of reading that he is mentally exhausted by the time he gets to the questions.

If he has a comprehension to do he can listen to the recording a number of times whilst he follows the text, and can concentrate on the questions without worrying about whether he has misread any of the words. He can work at his own pace without continually having to ask for help. This gives him a degree of independence, which is an important objective.

If notes on a chapter of History or Geography have to be made, a similar procedure can be followed. The tape can also be listened to in bed if there is to be a test the following day. With regard to set books for GCSE English, there are often commercial recordings available. Do watch out for what is on the radio; quite often books that are read at school are serialized.

A tape can also be used for questions and answers on almost any subject e.g. "what is a carbohydrate?", "what is CO_2?", "comment vous appelez-vous?". Allow a suitable pause for the answer to be given, and then give the answer. The tape can be practised over and over again in the privacy of your dyslexic's bedroom with no-one there to hear the mistakes. Once again, it encourages independence in learning.

ACTING AS SCRIBE

For a dyslexic to have to read the question, find the answer, remember it long enough to write it down, think about his handwriting, grapple with his spelling, put in the punctuation and arrange the work neatly on the page can cause 'overload'. Often, his coping strategy is to keep the answer or piece of writing as short as possible and to use 'safe' words, that is, those he can spell rather than the more imaginative ones that he is thinking, but can't spell. If the aim of the exercise is to test understanding or creative ability rather than the other items I have listed, then I think it perfectly reasonable to act as a scribe and to write down what your dyslexic dictates to you so that he can copy it out. Careful judgement must be used as to how much you correct what he says or what input you give to the creative process, as it should be his own work. However, I would always spell the words correctly, and would read the work back to him in the hope that he could spot some of the grammatical errors and know where to put the full stops. There is no point in his copying incorrectly spelled words, thus reinforcing his own mistakes.

After dictating to you he may need a break before he starts copying it out. The work may need to be completed in short bursts, depending on his concentration span.

It may well be diplomatic to discuss this approach with his teacher. This is why I mentioned at the beginning of the chapter that it is necessary to ascertain the purpose of the homework. Is it testing his reading ability, his spelling, his grammar, his understanding, his creative ability? If there are objections to your giving this kind of help, these are the points that need discussing. I'm not too happy with the comment: "I want to see what he can do." That should be evident from his classwork. I would rather see homework used for consolidation and rehearsal of what has been learned rather than a time for frustration and yet more failure.

EXAMINATIONS — SPECIAL PROVISION

It is possible for dyslexics to have special provision in public examinations such as GCSE, A levels, City and Guilds and RSA. The usual consideration is for up to 25% extra time to be allowed in written examinations. In extreme cases, a word processor can be used, an amanuensis may be supplied (that is, the student dictates the answers for someone else to write down), or the questions may be read to the candidate. The last three allowances would be granted only when this was the usual mode of working for the student.

All applications have to be supported by an educational psychologist's report that indicates that the candidate has a specific learning difficulty and that he would not be at an unfair advantage if such provisions were allowed. For the extreme cases requiring more than just extra time, a medical report may be required.

The specific arrangements for the allowances are subject to change and vary from board to board, so it is necessary to talk to your child's school about which board he will be sitting and when application has to be made. The psychologist's report is usually required within eighteen months of the final examinations so it is advisable to make enquiries at the beginning of the two-year course in order to give ample time to arrange for the required assessment.

The British Dyslexia Association keeps up-to-date on the requirements of the various examination boards, and they publish an excellent booklet.

Some students prefer not to have special arrangements made, as they want to 'go-it-alone', but for others the knowledge that they have fifteen minutes extra for each hour of examination can make an enormous difference. It gives them the opportunity to show what they have learned and how they can apply their knowledge and understanding, without being inhibited by their slow reading and writing speed or their need for extra time for proof-reading. Seeing your neighbour begin writing when you are only halfway through reading a passage is almost guaranteed to produce feelings of panic.

Jonathan was allowed the provision of extra time. He found, in the event, that he didn't use it for science-based subjects, especially those requiring multi-choice answers. However, he found it essential for English Language and English Literature as those examinations presented him with a considerable amount of reading.

CHAPTER 10

HOBBIES — THE POSSIBLE HAZARDS

SPORT

Encouraging hobbies and interests is very important but must be handled with sensitivity. There are activities that some dyslexics find quite difficult: games that involve hand-to-eye coordination can be a problem for some (not all — there are exceptions to every rule). Tennis, cricket and football may not be the best sports as they involve hitting a moving target. However, swimming, riding or long-distance running could prove ideal, as a different kind of co-ordination is required. Dancing can be a problem because of the necessity to learn sequences. (I never mastered cartwheels at ballet lessons, and I had problems with formation dancing at ballroom dancing lessons. Even today I can't remember sequences at my aerobics class, but have to watch the instructor all the time.) This is not to say that dyslexics shouldn't try these activities; they may be able to manage very well, but it would be best to watch the situation carefully to ensure that it is not creating additional stress and a further sense of failure.

Stress could also be caused if, for instance, Dad is a good cricketer and he tries to involve his dyslexic in his passion for the sport. This might work wonders for the father/son (daughter?) relationship, but on the other hand, it might cause yet further feelings of failure since the dyslexic might think he is not coming up to his father's expectations and is letting him down.

MUSIC

Learning a musical instrument is also fraught with pitfalls. Musical notation is a symbolic language and a dyslexic has already had difficulty with learning one symbolic language (i.e. the alphabet), and may well experience difficulties with another. Even if he does manage to get to grips with notation at a basic level, he has to learn to scan ahead, to look at one part of the music whilst playing another, to take notice of all the other symbols that indicate speed and dynamics, and so on. If he learns the piano he has to learn to read two staves of music simultaneously. (Not having been able to master this skill myself I am filled with admiration for those who do, and as for following a full orchestral score involving endless staves of music, I equate that skill with putting a man on the moon!) An additional complication with learning the piano is that whilst the two staves of music are moving from left to right with the notes going up and down the page, the hands may well be moving from right to left. For some dyslexics learning an instrument such as the trumpet may be the answer, as this involves just one hand and individual notes. (Any trumpeters reading this, please do not take offence: I am not decrying your skill and I know it is not as easy as that!)

Children can learn a number of instruments through the Suzuki method, which involves no reading of music initially. Alternatively, there are methods for colour-coding the notes. These can be marvellous ways to start, but there still comes a time when the switch to traditional notation becomes necessary in order to progress further.

As with sports, I am not saying that you shouldn't let your dyslexic have a go, but do tread carefully. It might be advisable to explain to your child's instrumental teacher the nature of dyslexia in order to avoid accusations of laziness or lack of practice, if learning the notation proves a struggle.

BOARD GAMES

In order to avoid playing Scrabble at my husband's home I took up embroidery and became quite good at it. Our home is full of cushion covers which were the result of my excuse for not joining in this Sunday afternoon pastime. ("Do you mind if I just watch, as I want to finish embroidering this daisy?")

Games that include spelling are obviously not popular with most dyslexics. Many board games and card games require one to remember what has gone before, or what the opponent has in his hand. This short-term memory activity can prove very taxing for the dyslexic, as can games with a general knowledge component; the "it's on the tip of my tongue" feeling is all too common because of the dyslexic's labelling/word retrieval difficulty.

Many dyslexics just get too fidgety if the game requires them to concentrate for a long time; they would rather be making something, or be out in the garden.

Much patience and understanding is necessary. I am all in favour of playing games with children (anything to stop so much television watching) but it might be best to start with games that involve a fair bit of luck and that do not take too long. Otherwise, so as not to annoy other members of the family who have more stickability, it might be best for the dyslexic to play with a partner, so that he can come and go when he gets the fidgets.

TELEVISION

What about television watching? I feel most children, not just dyslexics, watch far too much television. However, I know that Jonathan has picked up vast amounts of general knowledge from his viewing. Although now an avid reader of photographic magazines and Morris Minor car maintenance manuals, for many years he read nothing from choice. However, through watching science and nature programmes he has a wealth of knowledge and understanding about the world around him.

We have not exercised a great deal of censorship with regard to what our children have watched, although there was a time when we rationed how much they could watch. They had to look in the newspaper when they arrived home from school to work out which programmes they were going to watch, and they had to go and do something more constructive when their allocated time was up. As a family we have always discussed programmes and we have tried to help them distinguish between fantasy and reality. I think we have had some measure of success at helping them become discerning viewers as they now watch a healthy mixture of absolute rubbish and informative, serious and thought-provoking discussions and documentaries.

CHAPTER 11

CHOOSING A SCHOOL

I am sometimes asked for advice on choosing a school for a dyslexic. It is very difficult to suggest specific schools as it only takes a change of head teacher, or changes on the staff, and the whole character of a school can alter. I have also found that what suits one child will not suit another. On more than one occasion I have heard different parents discussing the same school and what it has done/not done for their child: they could have been describing quite different schools.

The first choice is whether to opt for the State-maintained sector or the Private (Independent) sector. With the ever-increasing cost of independent school education, the latter is not a viable proposition for most parents. There are some excellent specialist dyslexia schools or schools with dyslexia units in the private sector, but merely paying fees does not necessarily guarantee a better education. Certainly, independent schools will often have smaller classes, so that the teacher may give more help and attention to pupils with specific learning difficulties than is sometimes possible in larger classes.

Equal care must be taken, whether the choice is independent or state education. Whilst it is very difficult to recommend specific schools, it is possible to suggest the kind of questions to ask whilst looking around a school. It is advisable to visit more than one school so that comparisons can be made. Don't listen to what just one parent has to say about it: it might not be the right school for their child but it could be perfect for yours.

INDEPENDENT SCHOOLS

In the private sector the choice is between specialist schools, schools with a dyslexia unit, and schools with a specialist teacher on the staff. They all have their own advantages and disadvantages.

SPECIALIST SCHOOLS

Usually, specialist schools have very small classes for all subjects. The staff, whilst not all being dyslexia-trained teachers, will nevertheless be knowledgeable with regard to the learning needs of the dyslexic pupil. Even the matrons (these schools usually have boarding facilities) and the domestic staff will be aware of the organizational difficulties that plague the dyslexic. The obvious advantage of such a school is that the dyslexic is in a totally supportive environment. The disadvantage is that the dyslexic will not necessarily be given the opportunity to come to terms with his dyslexia in the context of a non-dyslexic world. For some, the advantages outweigh the disadvantages. In some instances the dyslexic attends such a school for no more than two years for intensive remedial help and then re-integrates into mainstream education.

DYSLEXIA UNITS

A school with a dyslexia unit can offer the advantage of involvement with non-dyslexic pupils whilst time-tabling specialist help on a regular basis. If such a school is being contemplated it is necessary to establish which lessons take place in the unit and which are attended with non-dyslexic pupils. The balance between the two arrangements will depend on the severity of your dyslexic's learning difficulties.

SPECIALIST TEACHERS

A school that offers help through the use of a specialist teacher can be a suitable choice if your dyslexic's difficulties are not too great. It would be advisable to check whether the teacher has a specific qualification for the teaching of dyslexics, as the skills that a remedial teacher has to offer are not always appropriate for the dyslexic. It would be necessary to ascertain what level of support is offered, whether timetabling necessitates the missing of favourite subjects (e.g. art, music, P.E.) and whether the dyslexic's needs are carefully monitored and the provision adjusted when necessary.

LISTS OF SCHOOLS

Council for the Registration of Schools Teaching Dyslexic Pupils (see p. 89), formed by a consortium comprising the British Dyslexia Association, the Dyslexia Institute and representatives of other voluntary and professional organisations, can supply a list of schools which offer specialist teaching.

STATE SCHOOLS — PARENTAL CHOICE

In the state-maintained sector, it is possible for parents to request that their child attend a school outside the catchment area in which they live, even if it is in another county. This gives greater choice for parents. Remedial provision, and in particular provision for dyslexic pupils, varies widely. It would be necessary to elicit information about the level of support given: is it arranged in a unit, on a withdrawal basis or as in-class support? What in-service training have the staff received with regard to learning difficulties (both for specialist and non-specialist teachers)? Is there a whole-school approach to the marking of spelling errors? (It can be very demoralising for a dyslexic to have answered all the science questions correctly but to have lost numerous marks for poor spelling.) Much can be learned about the philosophy of a school from the response to such questions.

DOES IT 'FEEL RIGHT'?

In the final analysis, the choice may depend on whether the school 'feels right'. Your instincts will probably tell you whether the school is a place where your child will be given the opportunity to fulfil his potential and where he will be happy (or relatively so!).

WITHDRAWAL

If your child attends an independent or a state school, and appropriate help is not available, lessons at a dyslexia unit such as the Dyslexia Institute (there are teaching centres and outposts throughout the country) or with a private tutor could be considered. All teachers employed by the Dyslexia Institute have completed a year's diploma course in specific learning difficulties. A private tutor may also have completed the Dyslexia Institute's diploma course, or an alternative course run by the Royal Society of Arts (RSA), the Hornsby Centre, the Helen Arkell Centre, or one of an increasing number of universities that are offering courses in specific learning difficulties.

Two lessons a week may be sufficient to develop the strategies your dyslexic needs to develop his literacy skills. These lessons may be arranged during the day or after school. Withdrawal from school is far from ideal, but if he is not receiving appropriate help, it is a matter of deciding on the lesser of the evils for a year or two: either he receives no help and continues to get further and further behind, or he misses some school so that he can catch up eventually.

CHAPTER 12

LOCAL SUPPORT GROUPS

KEEPING YOUR SANITY

As the parent of a dyslexic, if you want to keep your sanity I strongly recommend that you join your local Dyslexia Association.

THE BRITISH DYSLEXIA ASSOCIATION

Most support groups are affiliated to the British Dyslexia Association. This is a national organization with charitable status. Its function is to encourage and support the effective teaching of children and adults with specific learning difficulties, and to offer support to dyslexics and their families.

Local groups often have informal meetings where parents can share experiences and learn from each other's successes and failures.

TAKING COMFORT AND ADVICE

It can be very comforting to know that other parents are going through what you are experiencing, or better still, that they have gone through that particular trauma and survived! Many groups have more formal meetings with visiting speakers or they may run workshops where you can pick up useful tips for helping your dyslexic.

The committee members are usually a mine of information about the facilities available in the area, and will often give advice about liaising with schools and the local education authority. They may have members who act as 'befrienders' and will advise you about your rights as governed by various education acts, or will come with you into school if you find it difficult to talk to your child's headteacher.

If you can't find out from your library or the telephone directory who runs your nearest group, contact the British Dyslexia Association and they will put you in touch. If there isn't a group in your area, start your own. The BDA will tell you how.

FINDING OUT MORE

Overcoming Dyslexia By Dr Bevé Hornsby, published by Century Vermillion 1996. A 'must' for all teachers (not just special needs teachers). You could donate one to your child's school! Parents who would like to know more about the identification of dyslexia will find it compelling reading.

How to Detect and Manage Dyslexia by Philomena Ott, published by Heinemann Educational 1997. This offers an overview of all the issues relating to the identification and remediation of dyslexia. It is comprehensively referenced.

Children with Special Needs, Assessment, Law and Practice – Caught in the Act by John Friel, 4th edition published by Jessica Kingsley 1997. A 'must' for parents who seek guidance on the legal procedure for obtaining the education which their children need.

Help for the Dyslexic Adolescent by E.G.Stirling, published by St David's College 1987. (Available from Mrs Stirling, Tel: 01142 662286). Full of very practical study skills suggestions – probably designed more for teachers, unless your teenager likes you to help them with their homework.

Study Skills: A Pupil's Survival Guide by Christine Ostler, published by Ammonite Books 1996. In a practical and down-to-earth way this guide helps pupils who are disorganised but who would like to be more in control of their work. It encourages the student to discover their own preferred learning style, to become better organised and, above all, to get started.

Maths for the Dyslexic by Anne Henderson, published by David Fulton 1998. Detailed but very easy to follow.

What To Do When You Can't Learn Times Tables by Steve Chinn, published by Egon Publishers 1996. Also available on CDRom.

Use Your Head by Tony Buzan, published by BBC Books 1995, *Use Your Memory* also by Tony Buzan, published by BBC Books 1995, are fascinating books if you want to know more about the brain and memory.

Susan's Story by Susan Hampshire, published by Sidgwick & Jackson 1981. A heartwarming and encouraging autobiography of the famous actress.

Every Letter Counts by Susan Hampshire, published by Bantam. Interviews with famous dyslexics. Now out of print but worth tracking down.

Although I am wary about encouraging parents to teach their own child, if it works for you the following book has proved very successful for many parents: *Toe By Toe* by Keda Cowling, published by Toe by Toe 1993. A structured easy-to-follow word building manual for parent and child to read through together.

DICTIONARIES

Heinemann English Dictionary, published by Heinemann Educational 1995.

The Oxford Mini-Dictionary of Spelling, published by Oxford University Press 1997. Pocket-size – useful for words with suffixes.

Spelling Checklist by E.G.Stirling (Tel: 01142 662286). An alphabetical list of common words which dyslexics tend to mis-spell, with space for extra words to be added.

ACE Spelling Dictionary (Aurally Coded English) by David Moseley, published by Learning Developments Aids 1995. Words are found by using an index and cross-referencing the initial vowel sound and the initial letter of the word.

If you have difficulty in obtaining books relating to dyslexia the following offer excellent postal services:-

SEN Marketing (Colin & Rachel Redman), 618 Leeds Road, Outwood, Wakefield WF1 2LT (Tel: 01924 871697)

Better Books, 3 Paganel Drive, Dudley, West Midlands DY1 4AZ (Tel: 01384 253276)

USEFUL ADDRESSES

DYSLEXIA INSTITUTE
133 Gresham Road, Staines TW18 1SB
Tel: 01784 463851
A national teaching organization with centres throughout the country; assessment and teacher training available.

BRITISH DYSLEXIA ASSOCIATION
98 London Road, Reading RG1 5AU
Tel: Office 0118 966 2677, Helpline 0118 966 8271
A national pressure group which liaises with central and local government with the aim of protecting the rights of people with specific learning difficulties. It supports and encourages its members through its affiliated local Dyslexia Associations and teaching and assessment centres. It produces many useful publications including *Dyslexia, Your Questions Answered*, which is especially informative and easy to read.

THE HORNSBY INTERNATIONAL DYSLEXIA CENTRE
Glenshee Lodge, 261 Trinity Road, London SW18 3SN
Tel: 0181 874 1844.
Offers a comprehensive range of services including teaching, assessment and teacher training.

HELEN ARKELL DYSLEXIA CENTRE
Frensham, Farnham, Surrey GU10 3BW
Tel: 01252 792400
Offers teaching, study skills courses, assessment and teacher training.

COUNCIL FOR THE REGISTRATION OF SCHOOLS TEACHING DYSLEXIC PUPILS (CReSTeD)
Administrator: Mrs Christine Manser, Greygarth, Littleworth, Winchcombe, Cheltenham GL54 5BT Tel: 01242 602689
List of specialist schools.

IRLEN INSTITUTE
9 Orme Court, London W2 4RL (Tel: 0171 229 8810).
For information regarding coloured overlays and glasses.

DYSLEXIA SCHOOLS CONSULTANCY SERVICE
4 Arborfield Court, Arborfield Cross, Reading RG2 9JU
Tel: 01734 760362
Help for parents with choosing appropriate independent schools.

There are a number of other dyslexia centres offering excellent services covering assessment, teaching, teacher training and counselling. I have listed those with which I have personally had the most contact.

CHAPTER 13

IS IT ALL WORTH IT?

Is walking the tightrope between being a 'fussy parent' and being a 'concerned parent' worth it?

Is taking the time to help your dyslexic become better organized worth it?

Is maintaining a positive atmosphere in the face of the 'knife-in-the-stomach-slowly-twisting' situation worth it?

Is believing in your dyslexic against all odds worth it?

Yes! Yes, it really is.

This was brought home to me when Jonathan was thirteen. He had been on a ski-ing holiday with his school and on the return journey he found he had some French currency left. It was not sufficient for changing back into sterling, so he decided to spend it all. He looked ahead to the remainder of the journey and realized that they would be travelling up the M1 late at night and would not stop at a service station. He anticipated that his friends would become thirsty, so he spent his money on thirteen miniature cans of coke. Sure enough, things developed as he had anticipated, so he was able to sell the cans for 100% profit. It was at this point I stopped worrying about what the future might hold in store for Jonathan: with such organizing ability I decided he would survive!

If someone had told me when Jonathan was eight that he would gain eight GCSEs at grade C or above, I would not have believed them. It wasn't easy for him (or the family). He had to work very hard. There were tears, tantrums and black times, but with his teachers, the family, and Jonathan himself, all pulling in the same direction he was able to compensate for his learning difficulties and fulfil his potential.

This is not to say that all dyslexics should be aiming for seven, eight, nine GCSEs. Realistic expectations must be considered: what is appropriate for one pupil is not necessarily appropriate for another. However, no aim should be dismissed out of hand. Susan Hampshire's book 'Every Letter Counts' chronicles the lives of many well-known dyslexics who have achieved amazing goals against great odds. The key to success is determination, coupled with a willingness to work hard.

WHAT OF THE FUTURE?

Jonathan is just coming to the end of his first year at a college of education. He decided that, rather than take A levels, he would prefer to follow a more practically-based course. Consequently, he is taking a full-time two-year BTEC course in electronic and communication engineering. This has proved perfect for him. The course is designed so that every few weeks an assignment has to be handed in or a phase test has to be sat. The results go towards his final assessment. This well-organized structure is ideal for the dyslexic as it is essential for the student to keep up-to-date and to learn work for the regular tests. A dyslexic often finds it quite difficult to pace himself appropriately when following a two-year course with just one or two examinations at the end of it.

So far, Jonathan has done very well and, if he can maintain his high level of performance, he hopes later to take a degree in electronics.

What of Katharine and Nicholas? Katharine has had a year off before going to university to read psychology with a view to becoming an educational psychologist. She has been working as a class-room assistant with four to seven-year-olds. She has found she has a flair with children with learning difficulties! Undoubtedly, she has gained many insights into learning problems having grown up with a dyslexic brother. At the time of writing, Nicholas is in the middle of his GCSEs and is not really sure of what he would like to do. He has continued to develop very differently from his brother and quite likes the idea of becoming Literary Editor of *The Times*! Jonathan, who still prefers to make things rather than to read, finds this aspiration quite incomprehensible. How dull life would be if we were all the same. Vive la différence!

CHAPTER 14

POSTSCRIPT

Jonathan wasn't too keen about this piece of his early word processing being included, but I thought it appropriate for him to have the last word.

Experiences of My Childhood

Looking back now on my early life i almost wish i never had to grow up. No work, no obligations, and no responsibility.

I can trace my interest in electronics back to a very early age. I don't know how old i must have been but it seems likes a very long time. I used to break electrical appliances on a regular basis. My best trick was to knock over tables with TVs or radios on them. I then looked at all the interesting bits and bobs that fell out as the object smashed apart in front of me.

My other great hobby when I was a bit older was making tree houses and dugouts; my dugout consisted of a trench i had found in an over grown part of the school I live at. It was about four feet deep and six feet long by four feet wide; I enlarged it to six feet deep and covered it with wood and plastic from a dump area just in front of it and it had a sloping entrance.

My tree houses were built with great skill and with fearless enjoyment. I started with a plank of wood between two trees just six feet off the ground at an early age. They then progressed to twelve feet high platforms with roofs and at the height of my climbing life there was my best one yet. It was a secret one because my parents although they were very understanding of my dangerous hobbies they would not really like my last ever tree house. They knew I climbed the tree but did not know about the base at the top. The tree was just out side our house; it was as tall as our house. To get to the top you first walk up the trunk using a rope, then crawl along one of the larger branches to a rope ladder up this and the rest was easy hands and feet work. The use of this tree house and all trees is brought to a stop by one more of my great hobbies: going to hospital. This was one of my greatest skills and in my best year I had five to six operations, three of these accomplishments were what put me off climbing.

While on holiday I had managed to find myself flying through the air with great speed. I managed this by swinging on a rope over a sand slope and back to the top again. The rope was high up on a tree in a wood next to the sea; to cut along story short, my hands slipped off and I flew along then down. The flying was fine it was the ground that I could have handled better. As it was i had two broken wrists and did not climb for a year. This really marked the end of my early life and from then on I became more mature and I now try to break bones in a game called rugby.

Jonathan Ostler

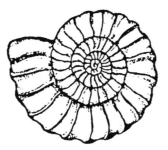

For full details of our publications please write to:

Ammonite Books
58 Coopers Rise
Godalming
Surrey GU7 2NJ

Also available by Christine Ostler:
Study Skills – A Pupil's Survival Guide